Criminalising Coercive Control

Drawing on experiences from other jurisdictions within the UK, *Criminalising Coercive Control* explores the challenges and potential successes which may be faced in implementing Northern Ireland's new domestic abuse offence.

A specific offence of domestic abuse was introduced in Northern Ireland in March 2021. This represents a crucial development in Northern Ireland's response to domestic abuse. The new legislation has the effect of criminalising coercive and controlling behaviour, thereby bringing Northern Ireland into line with other jurisdictions within the UK, and also with relevant human rights standards in this regard. The book begins with a discussion regarding the offence itself and the underpinning domestic abuse policy in Northern Ireland. Subsequent chapters explore further measures which may be needed to respond effectively to domestic abuse in Northern Ireland, by drawing upon the experiences of other jurisdictions of criminalising coercive control. These reflections are considered through the lenses of policing, prosecutorial practice and frontline domestic abuse working.

Criminalising Coercive Control will be of great interest to students and scholars in a variety of fields, such as criminal law, criminology, social policy, human rights, family law, gender studies and sociology. The book is also accessible beyond academia, including practitioners and those in the voluntary sector who are working in the area of combating domestic abuse.

Vanessa Bettinson is Professor of Criminal Law and Criminal Justice at De Montfort University, Leicester, UK. She researches coercive control in criminal law and is particularly interested in the creation and implementation of coercive control offences and embedding coercive control understandings within defence frameworks.

Ronagh McQuigg is a reader in the School of Law, Queen's University Belfast, UK. She holds an LLB with First Class Honours, an LLM with Distinction and a PhD, and she is a qualified solicitor. Her research interests focus in particular on domestic abuse, and she teaches in the areas of family law and property law.

Routledge Frontiers of Criminal Justice

Penal Abolitionism and Transformative Justice in Brazil
Andre R. Giamberardino

Impending Challenges to Penal Moderation in France and Germany
A Strained Restraint
Edited by Kirstin Drenkhahn, Fabien Jobard and Tobias Singelnstein

Narratives on Prison Governmentality
No Longer the Prison of the Past
Marco Nocente

Preventing Prison Violence
An Ecological Perspective
Armon J. Tamatea, Andrew J. Day and & David J. Cooke

European Perspectives on Pre-Trial Detention
A Means of Last Resort
Christine Morgenstern, Walter Hammerschick and Mary Rogan

War as Protection and Punishment
Armed Military Interventions at the 'End of History'
Teresa Degenhardt

Criminalising Coercive Control
Challenges for the Implementation of Northern Ireland's Domestic
Abuse Offence
Edited by Vanessa Bettinson and Ronagh McQuigg

For more information about this series, please visit: www.routledge.com/Routledge-Frontiers-of-Criminal-Justice/book-series/RFCJ

Criminalising Coercive Control

Challenges for the Implementation of Northern Ireland's Domestic Abuse Offence

Edited by Vanessa Bettinson and Ronagh McQuigg

LONDON AND NEW YORK

First published 2024
by Routledge
4 Park Square, Milton Park, Abingdon, Oxon OX14 4RN

and by Routledge
605 Third Avenue, New York, NY 10158

Routledge is an imprint of the Taylor & Francis Group, an informa business

© 2024 selection and editorial matter, Vanessa Bettinson and Ronagh McQuigg; individual chapters, the contributors

The right of Vanessa Bettinson and Ronagh McQuigg to be identified as the authors of the editorial material, and of the authors for their individual chapters, has been asserted in accordance with sections 77 and 78 of the Copyright, Designs and Patents Act 1988.

All rights reserved. No part of this book may be reprinted or reproduced or utilised in any form or by any electronic, mechanical, or other means, now known or hereafter invented, including photocopying and recording, or in any information storage or retrieval system, without permission in writing from the publishers.

Trademark notice: Product or corporate names may be trademarks or registered trademarks, and are used only for identification and explanation without intent to infringe.

British Library Cataloguing-in-Publication Data
A catalogue record for this book is available from the British Library

ISBN: 978-1-032-38487-0 (hbk)
ISBN: 978-1-032-38488-7 (pbk)
ISBN: 978-1-003-34530-5 (ebk)

DOI: 10.4324/9781003345305

Typeset in Times New Roman
by Apex CoVantage, LLC

Contents

List of Tables	*vi*
List of Contributors	*vii*

1 Introduction 1
VANESSA BETTINSON AND RONAGH MCQUIGG

2 Introducing a Criminal Offence of Domestic Abuse in Northern Ireland: Comparative Insights Into Criminalising Coercive Control 13
VANESSA BETTINSON AND RONAGH MCQUIGG

3 Understanding and Responding to Coercive Control: Lessons Learned From England and Wales 33
CHARLOTTE BARLOW

4 The Justice Challenge for Policing Northern Ireland: Training Police Officers in the Law of Control 50
ROB EWIN

5 Prosecuting Domestic Abuse in Northern Ireland: The Challenges of the Trial Process 65
JEREMY ROBSON

6 What Might 'Successful' Coercive Control Prosecutions Look Like? 81
ANTONIA PORTER

7 Taking Learnings From Other Jurisdictions on Supporting Victims and Survivors of Coercive Control 99
SONYA MCMULLAN

Index *113*

Tables

2.1 The elemental components of domestic abuse offences in the United Kingdom and the Republic of Ireland   18

Contributors

Charlotte Barlow is Reader in Criminal Justice and Policing at the University of Central Lancashire, UK, and Vice President of the British Society of Criminology. She researches violence against women and girls, in particular policing, criminal justice and legal responses to domestic abuse.

Vanessa Bettinson is Professor of Criminal Law and Criminal Justice at De Montfort University, Leicester, UK. She researches coercive control in criminal law and is particularly interested in the creation and implementation of coercive control offences and embedding coercive control understandings within defence frameworks.

Rob Ewin is currently the head of learning and development for Cumbria Constabulary, England. His research interests are mainly around the approaches of law enforcement to vulnerability, the law concerning victims and witnesses, and evidence-based practice. He also delivers and designs investigative leadership programmes, such as those available for deputy senior investigating officers, and learning and development programmes which relate to police activity around responses to domestic abuse, hotspot patrols and legalistic decision-making.

Sonya McMullan is the Regional Services Manager for Women's Aid Federation NI and has worked for Women's Aid in different roles since 1999. She previously managed the 24-Hour Domestic and Sexual Abuse Helpline and coordinated the development of the helpline to include sexual abuse. She holds a BSSc in Social Policy, an MSSc in Criminal Justice and Human Rights Law and a BLegSc in Legal Science.

Ronagh McQuigg is a reader in the School of Law, Queen's University Belfast, UK. She holds an LLB with First Class Honours, an LLM with Distinction and a PhD, and she is a qualified solicitor. Her research interests focus in particular on domestic abuse, and she teaches in the areas of family law and property law.

viii *Contributors*

Antonia Porter is a lecturer at the University of Kent, UK. She teaches Criminal Law, Criminal Justice and the Law of Evidence. She qualified as a solicitor in 2004 and has practised both as a criminal defence lawyer and as a senior crown prosecutor. She continues to be instructed as a trial advocate for the Crown Prosecution Service.

Jeremy Robson is an associate professor at De Montfort University, Leicester, UK, and a barrister, holding an Associate Tenancy at KCH Garden Square Chambers. His research interests revolve around the Law of Evidence and judicial decision-making. His particular focus is on how normative assumptions in the criminal justice system create barriers to justice.

1 Introduction

Vanessa Bettinson and Ronagh McQuigg

State responses to domestic abuse have been evolving at pace over the last decade. Several factors have contributed to this development including the introduction of the Council of Europe's Convention on preventing and combatting violence against women and domestic violence 2011 (also known as the Istanbul Convention), policy advances and legal reforms influenced by sociological understandings of domestic abuse, and campaigning by women's groups. In the United Kingdom, the legal landscape has been particularly impacted upon by these factors, culminating in new domestic abuse legislation in each jurisdiction. At the heart of legal change has been the recognition of wider behaviours used by abusers, and the serious effects of ongoing non-physical behaviours associated with domestic abuse upon victims, in criminal law frameworks. Such behaviours, alongside physical and sexual violence, are methods adopted by abusers who subject their victims to coercive control (Stark, 2007) and the question of criminalisation is now debated internationally (McMahon and McGorrery, 2020). Whilst Article 33 of the Istanbul Convention requires states to criminalise all forms of domestic abuse, traditional criminal law frameworks in the UK did not do so. Existing offences addressed single incidents, not identifying the pattern of criminal and non-criminal behaviours, the cumulative effect of which was to remove the autonomy of the victim. Moves to address this in the UK began in 2015 with section 76 of the Serious Crime Act 2015 (England and Wales), and continued with section 1 of the Domestic Abuse (Scotland) Act 2018. In March 2021, a new domestic abuse offence, which effectively criminalised coercive control, was enacted in Northern Ireland under section 1 of the Domestic Abuse and Civil Proceedings Act (Northern Ireland) 2021, and came into force on 21 February 2022. Introducing these offences has enabled the UK to finally ratify the Istanbul Convention, which entered into force there on 1 November 2022. Ratification illustrates the UK's commitment to combatting and preventing domestic abuse. Likewise in the Republic of Ireland, coercive control was criminalised under section 39 of the Domestic Violence Act 2018.

To mark the introduction of the domestic abuse offence in Northern Ireland, the editors organised an online event for academics, criminal justice professionals

DOI: 10.4324/9781003345305-1

2 *Vanessa Bettinson and Ronagh McQuigg*

and domestic abuse practitioners. Contributors were asked to highlight experiences of implementation in other jurisdictions in the UK and Ireland, providing opportunity for delegates to learn lessons and discuss challenges and solutions for the Northern Ireland legal system. Northern Ireland's move to criminalise all forms of domestic abuse is incredibly significant and brings its criminal justice system into alignment with other jurisdictions within the UK. It also means that non-physical forms of domestic abuse are criminalised across the island of Ireland. However, criminalisation of domestic abuse is not universally accepted (Goodmark, 2022). We acknowledge that the creation of new criminal offences is not a panacea for the phenomenon of domestic abuse. Without providing the funding for initiatives that support victims, appropriate interventions and preventions, domestic abuse will continue despite greater recognition in criminal law. As Goodmark highlights, expanding criminal justice responses can absorb the majority of state resources for domestic abuse services' infrastructure and can be a greater burden to victims of domestic abuse, for example, where police carry out dual arrests and fail to understand the protective strategies abused victims will use. Northern Ireland service providers will need to remain vigilant to any structural inequities that may compound the abuse experienced by victims and limit their access to justice. However, admitting that many issues will persist despite criminalising all forms of domestic abuse does not, in our opinion, make criminalisation unnecessary. In an educative role, new offences have provided the language needed in society to discuss the real experiences of domestic abuse victims, allowing for wider identification of such abuse by the public, victims and criminal justice personnel. The focus of this book is the examination of the criminalisation of domestic abuse in Northern Ireland, and the potential challenges of implementation by reflecting upon the experiences in England, Wales and Scotland.

This chapter examines the historical background in relation to domestic abuse in Northern Ireland, and discusses the importance of the criminalisation of coercive control in this jurisdiction. The structure of the book is then explained, and an outline of the forthcoming chapters is provided.

Responding to Domestic Abuse in Northern Ireland

Recognising domestic abuse as a legal issue at all in the UK is a relatively recent occurrence and as a criminal law issue more so (Burton, 2008). The United Nations Convention on the Elimination of All Forms of Discrimination Against Women 1981 (also known as CEDAW) did not provide official international legal recognition of domestic abuse as a gendered human rights issue until 1992, in its Committee's General Recommendation No. 19.[1] Traction for debating legal responses to domestic abuse was difficult in the context of Northern Ireland, exacerbated by the 'Troubles' which were very much a part of life from around the late 1960s until the late 1990s. As McWilliams and Ní Aoláin (2013, p. 27) explain, during this time, police resources were

Introduction 3

almost entirely focused on combating paramilitary activity. Little attention was therefore paid by the criminal justice system to issues such as domestic abuse.[2] In a study carried out by McWilliams and McKiernan in 1992, victims of domestic abuse frequently reported that police tended to minimise violence, side with perpetrators or refuse to intervene (McWilliams and McKiernan, 1993, p. 93). Few participants in the study reported that the police had taken official action (p. 92).

However, the Good Friday Agreement (or Belfast Agreement) was signed on 10 April 1998.[3] This Agreement formed the basis for Northern Ireland's current devolved system of government, and covered the creation of an Assembly, a North/South Ministerial Council, a British-Irish Council and a British-Irish Governmental Conference. A referendum on the Agreement was held on 22 May 1998, and 71.1% of those voting in Northern Ireland were in favour of its acceptance. The Northern Ireland Act 1998 was subsequently enacted in order to implement the Agreement. This Act set out the powers of the Assembly and the Executive as regards transferred, excepted and reserved matters. The Good Friday Agreement brought an end to a large amount, although not all, of Northern Ireland's political violence. The significance of this is once again under public scrutiny following the Northern Ireland Protocol and the Westminster Government's efforts to revisit it following the UK's departure from the European Union. The relative peace which followed the Good Friday Agreement meant that gradually more consideration was given to other issues, such as the suffering of victims of abuse taking place within their own homes.

A 'Tackling Violence at Home' regional strategy was launched in 2005 by the Northern Ireland Office and the Department of Health, Social Services and Public Safety.[4] In December 2010, Criminal Justice Inspection Northern Ireland (CJINI), which is the independent criminal justice inspectorate for this jurisdiction, issued a report on the handling of domestic abuse cases by the criminal justice system.[5] CJINI highlighted that improvements had been made since the 2005 strategy had been launched, including in relation to the specialisation of investigators and prosecutors, greater levels of engagement with the community and voluntary sector, and the rolling out of the Multi-Agency Risk Assessment Conference (MARAC) process. Nevertheless, CJINI was of the view that improvements were still necessary in order to provide greater support for victims.[6]

In March 2016, the Department of Health, Social Services and Public Safety and the Department of Justice issued a seven-year strategy on 'Stopping Domestic and Sexual Violence and Abuse in Northern Ireland'.[7] Part of this strategy focused on continually improving the protection and justice available to victims of abuse and their families. The strategy stated that in this regard, the identified priorities included that 'Focused protection, support and information will be available for all victims throughout their engagement with the Justice System'. In addition, 'Ongoing assessment of the capacity

4 *Vanessa Bettinson and Ronagh McQuigg*

of the Justice System to respond to current, new and emerging issues will be undertaken in relation to both the protection of victims, and in responding to harmful and violent behaviour'. Also prioritised was the need to 'continue to develop and deliver practices and interventions, based on best practice, to effectively address harmful, violent and abusive behaviour'.[8] Responses to domestic abuse in Northern Ireland had certainly improved by this time. It is notable that in a comparison of studies carried out in 1992 (McWilliams and McKiernan, 1993) and 2016 involving interviews with victims of domestic abuse, Doyle and McWilliams (2020, p. 148) found that the majority of participants in the 2016 study reported that their experiences with the police had been positive, with 62.5% of participants who had contacted the police describing them as 'helpful', 30% of participants describing them as 'not helpful' and the remaining 7.5% reporting 'mixed' experiences. By contrast, in the 1992 study, only 25.7% of participants had described the police as being 'helpful', with the remaining 74.3% of participants describing them as 'not helpful'. Also, in the 2016 study, most participants who had contacted the police said that official action had been taken, such as arresting the perpetrator (in 35% of cases) or issuing them with an official caution (in 32.5% of cases) (Doyle and McWilliams, 2020, pp. 149–150). As Doyle and McWilliams comment,

> While a number of other factors have undoubtedly contributed to improvements in policing of IPV (intimate partner violence), including local and global shifts in criminal justice and societal attitudes over the decades, what this research tells us is that the transition from violent conflict to peaceful political settlement plays a pivotal role.
>
> (p. 157)

Nevertheless, difficulties remained, particularly in relation to the lack of legislation criminalising coercive control. In the 2016 study discussed by Doyle and McWilliams, several participants reported that whilst the police responded in a helpful manner when an incident involved physical violence, 'they were often quite dismissive' when an incident involved psychological abuse (Doyle and McWilliams, 2020, p. 151). Such attitudes reflected the difficulties with the legislative framework under which domestic abuse was addressed. Northern Ireland's criminal law framework is drawn from such Acts of the Westminster Parliament which extend to this jurisdiction, legislation enacted by the Northern Ireland Assembly, legislation which was enacted by the Parliament of Northern Ireland which sat between 1921 and 1972, and Orders in Council. The Offences Against the Person Act 1861 applies to Northern Ireland, and incidents of domestic abuse in this jurisdiction had to be prosecuted under general criminal law statutes such as the 1861 Act. This was relatively unproblematic as regards incidents of physical violence, as these could be prosecuted under the 1861 Act as, for example,

Introduction 5

common assault under section 42, aggravated assault under section 43, assault occasioning actual bodily harm under section 47, assault occasioning grievous bodily harm under section 18, or unlawful wounding under section 20. However, broader patterns of coercive and controlling behaviour were not covered under the legislation.

By this time, the concept of coercive control[9] had emerged more strongly from sociological work to policy language, as more became known of the issue and realisation grew that existing laws were inadequate. As Herring (2020, p. 26) remarks, 'The concept of coercive control is an attempt to identify one of the wrongs at the heart of domestic abuse. It does so by showing that domestic abuse is a particular kind of relationship rather than being a particular kind of act'. Fitz-gibbon et al. (2018, p. 3) comment that 'Coercive control illuminates domestic abuse as a pattern of behaviours, within which physical violence may exist alongside a range of other abusive behaviours'. As Women's Aid states, 'Coercive control creates invisible chains and a sense of fear that pervades all elements of a victim's life. It works to limit their human rights by depriving them of their liberty and reducing their ability for action'.[10] As Herring (2020, p. 27) comments, 'Fear is often at the heart of coercive control and is its primary vehicle. Violence may or may not, be used as one tool'. For example, as is now recognised in section 2(3) of the Domestic Abuse and Civil Proceedings Act (Northern Ireland) 2021, coercive control may include making the victim dependent on, or subordinate to, the perpetrator. It may also include isolating the victim from friends, family members or other sources of social interaction or support; controlling, regulating or monitoring her day-to-day activities; restricting her freedom of action; or making her feel frightened, degraded or intimidated.[11] Additionally, coercive and controlling behaviour may include economic abuse relating to the victim's ability to acquire or use money or other property or to obtain goods or services.[12]

The necessity for the criminalisation of abuse capable of causing psychological harm has also been recognised in human rights standards. For example, Article 33 of the Istanbul Convention states that 'Parties shall take the necessary legislative or other measures to ensure that the intentional conduct of seriously impairing a person's psychological integrity through coercion or threats is criminalised'. Also, in *Volodina v Russia*,[13] the European Court of Human Rights recognised that the feelings of anxiety, fear and powerlessness which are caused by coercive and controlling behaviour can amount to inhuman treatment under Article 3 of the European Convention on Human Rights.[14] In addition, in its General Recommendation No. 19, the UN Committee on the Elimination of Discrimination Against Women (CEDAW Committee), the monitoring body of CEDAW, recognised that 'coercion' can amount to gender-based violence.[15] Prior to the enactment of the 2021 legislation, the fact that coercive control was not criminalised in Northern Ireland clearly fell short of human rights standards, and indeed in its 2019 Concluding Observations on the UK's eighth periodic report, the CEDAW

6 *Vanessa Bettinson and Ronagh McQuigg*

Committee expressed concern regarding the legislative position in relation to gender-based violence in Northern Ireland and recommended that the UK 'adopt legislative and comprehensive policy measures to protect women from all forms of gender-based violence throughout the State party's jurisdiction, including Northern Ireland'.[16]

Given the growing recognition that specific legislative steps are needed in order to respond adequately to the issue of domestic abuse, coercive and controlling behaviour was criminalised in England and Wales under section 76 of the Serious Crime Act 2015 (as amended by section 68 of the Domestic Abuse Act 2021). Abusive behaviour (construed extensively and inclusive of behaviour that amounts to coercive control) towards a partner or ex-partner was then criminalised in Scotland under section 1 of the Domestic Abuse (Scotland) Act 2018. In addition, coercive control was criminalised in the Republic of Ireland under section 39 of the Domestic Violence Act 2018.

It is notable that the definition of 'domestic violence and abuse' used in Northern Ireland's 2016 strategy encompassed 'threatening, controlling, coercive behaviour, violence or abuse (psychological, virtual, physical, verbal, sexual, financial or emotional)'.[17] Furthermore, it was stated that 'Domestic violence and abuse is generally recognised as a pattern of behaviour which is characterised by the exercise of coercive control and the misuse of power by one person over another'.[18] The strategy therefore recognised a wide range of harms and behaviours that arise in the domestic abuse context, and noted that the Department of Justice was at that time undertaking a consultation on protecting victims further by creating an offence to capture patterns of coercive and controlling behaviour.[19] By 2016, it had therefore been recognised in Northern Ireland that domestic abuse encompasses not only physical violence but also 'coercive control' more broadly.

In February 2016, the Department of Justice launched a public consultation on domestic abuse which included the question of whether a specific offence capturing coercive and controlling behaviour should be enacted.[20] Overwhelmingly, respondents were of the view that the current criminal law needed to change in order to recognise domestic abuse in all its forms. It was believed that 'Creating an offence would be a positive step towards ensuring that certain types of abuse are not overlooked or treated less seriously', and it was suggested that the offence should encompass mental, emotional and financial control.[21] Respondents highlighted the fact that the criminal justice system treated and, where appropriate, prosecuted each occurrence of domestic abuse as an individual incident, which meant that the cumulative effect of coercive and controlling behaviour was overlooked. The failure to take the repetition of such acts into consideration meant that the criminal law did not provide effective protection for victims.[22] Respondents also said that perpetrators who used coercive control may seek to justify their behaviour on the ground that it was non-violent. It was therefore noted that, as well as providing better protection for victims, a domestic abuse offence would send out a strong message to perpetrators that all forms of abuse are unacceptable and would have serious consequences.[23] In addition, a number of respondents highlighted the need for a strong sentencing regime that reflected the seriousness of domestic abuse.[24] Some respondents also expressed concerns that prosecuting cases of coercive and controlling behaviour could be difficult, particularly in relation to the gathering of sufficient evidence, and it was thus suggested that innovative approaches to evidence gathering should be considered.[25] It was noted that an offence should encapsulate situations in which ex-partners were continuing to exert coercive and controlling behaviour, even following separation.[26] Legislation criminalising coercive control was subsequently drafted for Northern Ireland, however, the passage of this stalled due to the suspension of the Northern Ireland Assembly from January 2017 until January 2020.[27]

Upon the restoration of the Assembly in January 2020, the Justice Minister, Naomi Long MLA, made the progression of legislation on domestic abuse a key priority of her department.[28] A specific offence of domestic abuse was introduced in Northern Ireland in March 2021 under section 1 of the Domestic Abuse and Civil Proceedings Act (Northern Ireland) 2021, and came into force on 21 February 2022.[29] This represents a crucial development in Northern Ireland's legal response to domestic abuse. The new legislation has the effect of criminalising coercive and controlling behaviour, thereby bringing Northern Ireland into line with other jurisdictions within the UK and Ireland, and with relevant human rights standards in this regard. Being the final jurisdiction within the UK and Ireland to criminalise such behaviour has enabled Northern Ireland's approach to be informed by the legislation enacted in other jurisdictions. However, although the enactment of the domestic abuse offence is certainly a very positive development, challenges may arise in relation to its implementation.

There have also been other important developments in Northern Ireland's response to domestic abuse. For example, a Domestic Violence and Abuse Disclosure Scheme (DVADS) commenced in Northern Ireland in March 2018. This scheme provides individuals with the 'Right to Ask' the Police Service of Northern Ireland (PSNI) to check if their partner, or the partner of someone they know, has a history of domestic abuse; as well as affording the PSNI the 'Power to Tell' an individual about their partner's abusive history. In March 2019, it was reported that over 326 applications had been made to the DVADS during its first year of operation, resulting in 40 people being advised regarding the abusive past of their partners.[30] Additionally, domestic homicide reviews were introduced in Northern Ireland in December 2020. Under section 9 of the Domestic Violence, Crime and Victims Act 2004, a domestic homicide review is a review of the circumstances in which the death of a person aged 16 or over has, or appears to have, resulted from violence, abuse or neglect by a person to whom they were related; a person with whom they were, or had been, in an intimate personal relationship; or a member of the

8 *Vanessa Bettinson and Ronagh McQuigg*

same household. The purpose of a domestic homicide review is to identify lessons which can be learnt from the death. As the Justice Minister commented, 'Domestic Homicide Reviews will illuminate the past to make the future safer for those who may be at risk or who are being subjected to domestic abuse'.[31] Furthermore, it has been found that most stalking offences are committed by abusive ex-partners[32]; and in April 2022, the Protection from Stalking Act (Northern Ireland) 2022 created an offence of stalking and also an offence of threatening and abusive behaviour. Additionally, there is a strong connection between non-fatal strangulation and domestic abuse, and an offence of non-fatal strangulation or asphyxiation was also enacted in April 2022 under section 28 of the Justice (Sexual Offences and Trafficking Victims) Act (Northern Ireland) 2022.[33]

Book Structure and Chapter Outline

Drawing on experiences from elsewhere in the UK, this book seeks to explore the challenges and potential successes which may be faced in implementing Northern Ireland's new domestic abuse offence. To do this, the book begins with a discussion regarding the offence itself and the underpinning domestic abuse policy in Northern Ireland. Subsequent chapters explore further measures which may be needed to respond effectively to domestic abuse in Northern Ireland. These reflections are considered through the lenses of policing, prosecutorial practice and frontline domestic abuse working. A balance of perspectives is provided, encompassing those from academia, legal practice and frontline working.

In Chapter 2, Vanessa Bettinson and Ronagh McQuigg analyse the new criminal law offence of domestic abuse in Northern Ireland. The authors reflect on whether the offence will succeed in strengthening this jurisdiction's response to domestic abuse. This analysis draws upon models designed for the same purpose in England and Wales, Scotland and Ireland, to assess where Northern Ireland may succeed or be challenged when operationalising the new offence. Through this comparison, the authors consider whether Northern Ireland has produced an offence model that has benefited from learning the lessons of other jurisdictions within the UK and Ireland.

The next part of the book focuses on lessons in policing. In Chapter 3, Charlotte Barlow explores police responses to coercive control. The chapter considers how the idea of coercive control is utilised, responded to and understood in practice by police officers in England and Wales, and the lessons which can be learnt as regards the implementation of Northern Ireland's domestic abuse offence. The chapter compares police officers' perceptions to the lived experiences of victims, exploring the ways in which opportunities for identifying and understanding the harms of coercive control have often been missed by police officers. The chapter concludes with a discussion of the

Introduction   9

limits of criminalisation approaches in providing safety for victims, advocating the need for holistic policy responses in Northern Ireland.

In Chapter 4, Rob Ewin discusses training police officers in the law of coercive control. As police and prosecutors in Northern Ireland seek to establish a safe and best working procedure for prosecutions surrounding coercive control, there are a number of challenges to overcome. One of these challenges is recognising the often-subtle nature of control which can take time to evolve – a one-time blue light response at a brief intersection in time and space could potentially limit what may appear on the prosecutor's desk as a viable case to put to the court. This chapter discusses some of the challenges around this police–prosecutor relationship and explores the advantages in using evidence-led and victim-motivated approaches as opposed to other traditional approaches which may revolve around the victim alone. The acceptance of evidence-led prosecutions, which may not be supported by victims, has variable success and the appetite to deploy these strategies is dependent on resources, practitioner knowledge and an acceptance of presentation of a case where the victim provides little evidence. This chapter provides case law and practice examples from England and Wales in an attempt to promote the 'plan B' option of securing prosecutions in coercive control cases.

The book then proceeds to focus on prosecutorial practice. In Chapter 5, Jeremy Robson looks at the need to 'reshape the trial' with regard to prosecuting coercive control in Northern Ireland. The successful implementation of a policy of criminalising coercive control requires a recognition that the trial process has evolved around the notion of determining individual factual disputes. The prosecution of coercive control requires the prosecution to be able to present a narrative which may span a considerable time period. Rules of evidence which have evolved to prove individual incidents may not so readily accommodate an offence which has taken place over time. The trial process may not also be fully equipped to deal with the nature of coercive behaviour. Drawing on experiences from England and Wales, this chapter examines the changes to rules of procedure and evidence which need to be considered alongside the introduction of the new criminal offence in Northern Ireland.

In Chapter 6, Antonia Porter considers what barriers exist for prosecutors when making the decision to charge and proceed with coercive control cases. Such barriers include the evidential (realistic prospect of conviction) obstacle, and the criminal trial's usual focus on discrete, incident-specific or 'transactional' offences. Set against this, offences concerning ongoing patterns and systems of power seem ill-fitted. Nevertheless, the chapter reminds prosecutors in Northern Ireland that what constitutes a successful outcome for a survivor of coercive control may go beyond committed implementation of the substantive criminal law and rules of evidence. Ultimately, taking domestic abuse 'seriously' for victims may not align with prosecution performance measurements and headline statistics and may require a cultural shift away from typical criminal justice paradigms.

10 *Vanessa Bettinson and Ronagh McQuigg*

The final section of the book focuses on frontline working. Chapter 7 is contributed by Sonya McMullan from the Women's Aid Federation Northern Ireland. Women's Aid campaigned for an offence of coercive control to be enacted in Northern Ireland for many years. During this time, the organisation highlighted the need for an offence to focus on the impact that coercive and controlling behaviours can have not only on the victim but on the whole family. The chapter examines how victims of coercive control in Northern Ireland can best be supported, and how training for relevant professionals can be developed to change culture and practice and to inform how devastating coercive and controlling behaviours can be for individuals and society as a whole.

Notes

1 Committee on the Elimination of Discrimination Against Women, General Recommendation No. 19: Violence Against Women (1992), para. 4.
2 For further discussion of domestic abuse in Northern Ireland during this time, see McWilliams and McKiernan (1993) and Evason (1982).
3 The Agreement can be accessed at https://assets.publishing.service.gov.uk/government/uploads/system/uploads/attachment_data/file/136652/agreement.pdf.
4 Department of Health and Social Services and Northern Ireland Office, 'Tackling Domestic Violence – A Policy for Northern Ireland', 1995.
5 Criminal Justice Inspection Northern Ireland, 'Domestic Violence and Abuse', December 2010, www.cjini.org/getattachment/1b651b43-657b-471b-b320-101fca7c6930/Domestic-Violence-and-Abuse.aspx.
6 Criminal Justice Inspection Northern Ireland, op. cit., at vii.
7 Department of Health, Social Services and Public Safety and Department of Justice, 'Stopping Domestic and Sexual Violence and Abuse in Northern Ireland – A Seven Year Strategy', March 2016, www.justice-ni.gov.uk/sites/default/files/publications/doj/stopping-domestic-sexual-violence-ni.pdf.
8 Department of Health, Social Services and Public Safety and Department of Justice, op. cit., at 63.
9 For discussion of the concept of coercive control, see Stark (2007), Stark (2009), Hanna (2009), Stark (2012), Tolmie (2018) and Stark and Hester (2019).
10 Women's Aid, 'What is Coercive Control?', www.womensaid.org.uk/information-support/what-is-domestic-abuse/coercive-control/.
11 See also section 2(3) of the Domestic Abuse (Scotland) Act 2018.
12 As noted in section 4(3)(a)(i) of the Domestic Abuse and Civil Proceedings Act (Northern Ireland) 2021.
13 Application no. 41261/17, judgement of 9 July 2019, para. 75.
14 Article 3 states that 'No one shall be subjected to torture or to inhuman or degrading treatment or punishment'.
15 Committee on the Elimination of Discrimination Against Women, General Recommendation No. 19: Violence Against Women (1992), para. 6.
16 Committee on the Elimination of Discrimination Against Women, 'Concluding observations on the eighth periodic report of the United Kingdom of Great Britain and Northern Ireland', CEDAW/C/GBR/CO/8 (14 March 2019) para. 30(b).
17 Department of Health, Social Services and Public Safety and Department of Justice, op. cit., at 3.

Introduction 11

18 Department of Health, Social Services and Public Safety and Department of Justice, op. cit., at 18.
19 Department of Health, Social Services and Public Safety and Department of Justice, op. cit., at 60.
20 Department of Justice, 'Domestic Abuse Offence and Domestic Violence Disclosure Scheme – A Consultation', 5 February 2016, www.justice-ni.gov.uk/sites/default/files/consultations/doj/consultation-domestic-violence.PDF.
21 Department of Justice, 'Domestic Abuse Offence and Domestic Violence Disclosure Scheme – A Consultation, Summary of Responses', 2016, www.justice-ni.gov.uk/sites/default/files/consultations/justice/domestic-abuse-offence-domestic-violence-disclosure-scheme-summary-of-responses.pdf, para. 1.9.
22 Department of Justice, 'Domestic Abuse Offence and Domestic Violence Disclosure Scheme – A Consultation, Summary of Responses' (2016), op. cit., at para. 1.10.
23 Department of Justice, 'Domestic Abuse Offence and Domestic Violence Disclosure Scheme – A Consultation, Summary of Responses' (2016), op. cit., at para. 1.11.
24 Department of Justice, 'Domestic Abuse Offence and Domestic Violence Disclosure Scheme – A Consultation, Summary of Responses' (2016), op. cit., at para. 1.12.
25 Department of Justice, 'Domestic Abuse Offence and Domestic Violence Disclosure Scheme – A Consultation, Summary of Responses' (2016), op. cit., at para. 1.13.
26 Department of Justice, 'Domestic Abuse Offence and Domestic Violence Disclosure Scheme – A Consultation, Summary of Responses' (2016), op. cit., at para. 1.14.
27 See BBC News, 'New abuse law "held up by lack of NI Assembly"', 19 January 2018, www.bbc.co.uk/news/uk-northern-ireland-42739589.
28 Northern Ireland Assembly, 'Official Report: Tuesday 28 April 2020', Naomi Long MLA, Justice Minister.
29 The Domestic Abuse and Civil Proceedings Act (Northern Ireland) 2021 (Commencement No. 1) Order (Northern Ireland) 2022.
30 Northern Ireland Executive, '326 checks carried out in the last year through the Domestic Violence and Abuse Disclosure Scheme', 26 March 2019, www.northernireland.gov.uk/news/326-checks-carried-out-last-year-through-domestic-violence-and-abuse-disclosure-scheme.
31 Department of Justice (2020), op. cit.
32 Crown Prosecution Service, 'Stalking analysis reveals domestic abuse link', 4 December 2020, www.cps.gov.uk/cps/news/stalking-analysis-reveals-domestic-abuse-link.
33 For further discussion of non-fatal strangulation and domestic abuse, see Bettinson (2022).

References

Bettinson, V. (2022) 'A Comparative Analysis of Non-Fatal Strangulation Offences: Will the Proposed s. 75A Serious Crime Act 2015 Work for Victims of Domestic Violence and Abuse?', *The Journal of Criminal Law*, 86, pp. 75–93.

Burton, M. (2008) *Legal Responses to Domestic Violence*. Abingdon: Routledge.

Doyle, J.L. and McWilliams, M. (2020) 'What Difference Does Peace Make? Intimate Partner Violence and Violent Conflict in Northern Ireland', *Violence against Women*, 26, pp. 139–163.

Evason, E. (1982) Hidden Violence: Battered Women in Northern Ireland. Belfast: Farset Cooperative Press.

Fitz-gibbon, K., Walklate, S. and McCulloch, J. (2018) 'Editorial Introduction', *Criminology and Criminal Justice*, 18, pp. 3–6.

12 *Vanessa Bettinson and Ronagh McQuigg*

Goodmark, L. (2022) 'Assessing the Impact of the Violence against Women Act', *Annual Review of Criminology* 5, pp. 115–131.

Hanna, C. (2009) 'The Paradox of Progress: Translating Evan Stark's Coercive Control into Legal Doctrine for Abused Women', *Violence against Women*, 15, pp. 1458–1476.

Herring, J. (2020) *Domestic Abuse and Human Rights*. Cambridge: Intersentia.

McMahon, M. and McGorrery, P. (2020) *Criminalising Coercive Control: Family Violence and the Criminal Law*. Singapore: Springer.

McWilliams, M. and McKiernan, J. (1993) *Bringing It Out in the Open: Domestic Violence in Northern Ireland*. Belfast: HMSO.

McWilliams, M. and Ní Aoláin, F. (2013) '"There Is a War Going on You Know": Addressing the Complexity of Violence against Women in Conflicted and Post Conflict Societies', *Transitional Justice Review*, 1, pp. 4–44.

Stark, E. (2007) *Coercive Control: How Men Trap Women in Personal Life*. Oxford: Oxford University Press.

Stark, E. (2009) 'Rethinking Coercive Control', *Violence against Women*, 15, pp. 1509–1525.

Stark, E. (2012) 'Looking Beyond Domestic Violence: Policing Coercive Control', *Journal of Police Crisis Negotiations*, 12, pp. 199–217.

Stark, E. and Hester, M. (2019) 'Coercive Control: Update and Review', *Violence against Women*, 25, pp. 81–104.

Tolmie, J.R. (2018) 'Coercive Control: To Criminalize or Not to Criminalize?', *Criminology and Criminal Justice*, 18, pp. 50–66.

2 Introducing a Criminal Offence of Domestic Abuse in Northern Ireland

Comparative Insights Into Criminalising Coercive Control

Vanessa Bettinson and Ronagh McQuigg

This chapter analyses the new criminal law offence of domestic abuse in Northern Ireland, which seeks to criminalise coercive and controlling behaviour. The chapter reflects on whether the offence will succeed in strengthening this jurisdiction's response to domestic abuse. This analysis draws upon models designed for the same purpose in England and Wales, Scotland and the Republic of Ireland, to assess where Northern Ireland may succeed or be challenged when operationalising the new offence. Through this comparison, the chapter considers whether Northern Ireland has produced an offence model that has benefited from learning the lessons of other jurisdictions within the UK and Ireland.

Whilst Northern Ireland is the last jurisdiction in the United Kingdom to introduce a domestic abuse offence with the purpose of criminalising coercive control, the Department of Justice launched a public consultation on this issue in 2016.[1] This was shortly after England and Wales introduced section 76 Serious Crime Act 2015. The long journey from consultation to legislation was less about government's willingness to legislate and more a consequence of broader political factors in Northern Ireland, which culminated in the suspension of the Northern Ireland Assembly between January 2017 and January 2020.[2] The time lost on the one hand is regrettable as noted in Chapter 1. However, at this time, Northern Ireland had the benefit of learning from the developments in other jurisdictions. When Scotland introduced section 1 Domestic Abuse (Scotland) Act 2018, the structure of its domestic abuse offence differed significantly from section 76 Serious Crime Act 2015 and was closely aligned to its own policy approaches (Bettinson, 2016). In doing so, Scotland had provided an alternative option in terms of drafting an offence that predated Northern Ireland's domestic abuse offence. Similarly, in the Republic of Ireland, section 39 Domestic Violence Act 2018 offered a further model of a domestic abuse offence. Conducting comparative analysis can be valuable to the legislature seeking to design their

DOI: 10.4324/9781003345305-2

14 *Vanessa Bettinson and Ronagh McQuigg*

own offences, and the practitioner seeking to implement laws. As Wilson (2017, p. 164) observes, comparative research can

> benefit the national legal system of the observer, offering suggestions for future developments, providing warnings of possible difficulties, giving an opportunity to stand back from one's own national system and look at it more critically, but not to remove it from first place on the agenda.

The comparative exploration in this chapter will focus on the elemental components of the offences in each of the four jurisdictions. This will determine any challenges and opportunities that may arise in the implementation of the offences and consequently highlight the need for specialist training of criminal justice personnel, and the importance of partnership working between statutory agencies and domestic abuse frontline services in Northern Ireland.

Context

As was discussed in Chapter 1, prior to the passing of the Domestic Abuse and Civil Proceedings Act (Northern Ireland) 2021, the legislative position as regards domestic abuse in Northern Ireland was problematic. Essentially, there was no specific offence of domestic abuse in this jurisdiction. Coercive control was not criminalised, a situation which failed to comply with relevant human rights standards, such as Article 33 of the Council of Europe's Convention on preventing and combatting violence against women and domestic violence 2011 (also known as the Istanbul Convention). However, given the growing recognition that specific legislative steps were needed in order to respond adequately to the issue of domestic abuse, coercive and controlling behaviour had been criminalised in England and Wales under section 76 of the Serious Crime Act 2015 (as amended by section 68 of the Domestic Abuse Act 2021). Abusive behaviour (construed extensively and inclusive of behaviour that amounts to coercive control) towards a partner or ex-partner had then been criminalised in Scotland under section 1 of the Domestic Abuse (Scotland) Act 2018, and coercive control had been criminalised in the Republic of Ireland under section 39 of the Domestic Violence Act 2018.

In 2016, the Department of Justice Northern Ireland launched a public consultation on whether a specific offence of coercive and controlling behaviour should be enacted.[3] Responses were overwhelmingly in the affirmative, with respondents making the point that the introduction of such an offence would be a positive step which would clearly indicate that domestic abuse in all its forms would not be tolerated in society. Respondents were also of the view that the creation of a specific offence would give the police the opportunity to intervene at an early stage, prior to the occurrence of physical violence, thus potentially preventing domestic abuse from escalating.[4] Eventually,

Criminal Offence of Domestic Abuse in Northern Ireland 15

legislation criminalising coercive control was subsequently drafted for Northern Ireland, following delays due to the suspension of the Northern Ireland Assembly.[5] This meant that, until March 2021, Northern Ireland was the only jurisdiction within the UK and Ireland in which coercive control was not criminalised. This position, in part, was the reason the UK delayed ratification of the Istanbul Convention, as non-criminalisation of psychological harm in abusive relationships would be incompatible with Article 33.

Upon the restoration of the Northern Ireland Assembly in January 2020, securing the enactment of such legislation became a key priority of the Department of Justice Northern Ireland[6] and on 31 March 2020 the Domestic Abuse and Family Proceedings Bill was introduced in the Assembly. This legislation subsequently received Royal Assent on 1 March 2021 as the Domestic Abuse and Civil Proceedings Act (Northern Ireland) 2021,[7] entering into force on 21 February 2022.[8] The Explanatory and Financial Memorandum to the Bill stated that the introduction of an offence of domestic abuse would give effect 'to the intention to improve the operation of the justice system by creating an offence that recognises the experience of victims, the repetitive nature of abusive behaviour and the potential cumulative effect of domestic abuse'.[9] The purpose of the new offence was to 'enabl[e] a range of domestic abuse incidents, which take place over a period of time, to be prosecuted as a single course of behaviour within a new offence' with the criminal law better reflecting 'how victims actually experience such abuse'.[10] Criminalisation does have an educative role explaining to society what will and will not be condoned and in doing so can articulate the prohibited behaviour and the harm it causes (Bettinson and Bishop, 2015). The mere existence of a criminal offence cannot achieve this in isolation as it requires successful implementation, which relies on the actors responsible for investigating and prosecuting crimes and consequently, concerns have been expressed about the abilities of the law to achieve better outcomes for victims of domestic abuse (Tolmie, 2018).

The Offence

The Northern Irish offence adopts an aspect of the English and Welsh model, although for the most part mirrors the Scottish model, signifying that the drafting was influenced by comparative jurisdictions, and could have capitalised on lessons learnt from them in terms of operationalising it.

Section 1(1) Domestic Abuse and Civil Proceedings Act (Northern Ireland) 2021 states that:

A person ('A') commits an offence if –

(a) A engages in a course of behaviour that is abusive of another person ('B'),
(b) A and B are personally connected to each other at the time, and
(c) both of the further conditions are met.

16 *Vanessa Bettinson and Ronagh McQuigg*

Under section 1(2), the further conditions are:

(a) that a reasonable person would consider the course of behaviour to be likely to cause B to suffer physical or psychological harm, and
(b) that A –

    (i) intends the course of behaviour to cause B to suffer physical or psychological harm, or
    (ii) is reckless as to whether the course of behaviour causes B to suffer physical or psychological harm.

The legislation is intended to allow characteristics that further a victim's vulnerability to be considered by the court, as highlighted by the Financial and Explanatory Memorandum to the Bill:

> The court would be entitled to take account of the circumstances of the case, for example any particular vulnerability of the partner/connected person, in considering whether the accused's behaviour would be likely to cause them to suffer physical or psychological harm.[11]

This is important as factors such as age, sexuality, religion, race and immigration status can be used by the perpetrator to increase their control of the victim and impact the institutional response to them (Douglas et al., 2021).

The format of the domestic abuse offences introduced in England, Wales and Scotland reflected their own policy approaches towards domestic abuse, which differed in several ways. One significant way was in the definition of domestic violence and abuse, with England and Wales extending the term to include both intimate partners and family members, and Scotland restricting it exclusively to intimate partners. Likewise, in including both intimate partners and family members, Northern Ireland also followed its own policy approach, in that the seven-year strategy on 'Stopping Domestic and Sexual Violence and Abuse' issued by the Department of Health, Social Services and Public Safety and the Department of Justice in March 2016 defined domestic violence and abuse as encompassing both intimate partners and family members.[12] As Bettinson suggests, replicating policy approaches in each jurisdiction in the domestic abuse offences is sensible, as it provides a better chance of implementing the law successfully. Those bound by policy approaches are able to extend their learnt practice when applying the law, reducing confusion or creating conflicting policy and legal approaches (Bettinson, 2016).

This chapter will now explore the variations of each domestic abuse offence in England and Wales, Scotland, the Republic of Ireland and Northern Ireland. Rather than determining which model is the most progressive, the focus will be on establishing how the Northern Ireland offence could be successfully implemented or inhibited. This will be achieved through a comparative

Criminal Offence of Domestic Abuse in Northern Ireland 17

reflection of the elemental components of the domestic abuse offences and consideration of obstacles or opportunities that have arisen in regard to these components in each jurisdiction. Table 2.1 illustrates the key components of the domestic abuse offences which are required to secure a conviction.

Abusive Behaviour

All the jurisdictions discussed in this chapter recognise single acts of physical harm under general non-fatal offences. However, the inadequacies of these offences in the context of domestic abuse arise from their focus on single incidents, making the context in which they took place irrelevant to the purpose of proving them (Wiener, 2020). The invisibility of the reality of a victim's experiences throughout the criminal justice process is increased as only physical harm is considered and not the ongoing pattern of coercive control characterised by both physical and non-physical behaviour by the perpetrator (Bettinson and Bishop, 2015). Verbal behaviour that causes a degree of psychological harm is limited to the minor offence of assault, and where the harm is greater, psychiatric injury, not mere emotions, must be proven (for example, in R v Chan Fook [1994] 1 WLR 689). Harassment laws offered an opportunity for prosecutors to connect more than one incident of harassing behaviour (section 1 Protection from Harassment Act 1997/Articles 3 and 6 Protection from Harassment (Northern Ireland) Order 1997) together into a more serious charge. However, this proved ineffective for domestic abuse cases in England and Wales through restrictive judicial interpretation (R v Hills [2001] Crim LR 318). In Scotland, sections 38 and 39 Criminal Justice and Licensing (Scotland) Act 2010 were capable of applying to domestic abuse cases, but were criticised for not requiring a consideration of the domestic abuse context in which the abusive behaviour occurred (Bettinson, 2016). Following a consultation on the question of whether a specific domestic abuse offence should be introduced, the majority of respondents answered in the affirmative, with the view that it would improve the way the criminal justice system responds to domestic abuse.[13] Likewise, in Northern Ireland, respondents to the Department of Justice's 2016 consultation on domestic abuse were overwhelmingly of the view that the current criminal law needed to change in order to recognise domestic abuse in all its forms.[14]

Embarking upon a new offence that seeks to articulate the experiences of victims of domestic abuse means that defining the behaviour concerned ought to be a key priority. For England and the Republic of Ireland however, this does not seem to have been the case. Both jurisdictions describe the prohibited behaviour as coercive or controlling, emphasising the influence of a sociological construct (Wiener, 2020) brought to recent prominence by Stark (2007). Neither provided legislative definitions for controlling or coercive behaviour at the time the provisions were enacted. Consequently, this undermines the key aim of articulating forms of domestic abuse not previously captured by

Table 2.1 The elemental components of domestic abuse offences in the United Kingdom and the Republic of Ireland

Jurisdiction	Frequency	Behaviour	Relationship	Harm	Mens rea
England and Wales *Serious Crime Act 2015* (UK) s 76	Repeatedly or continuously	Controlling or coercive Explained in statutory guidance	The defendant and the victim are personally connected, which includes being in an intimate relationship, or living together and either (i) being members of the same family or (ii) having previously been in an intimate relationship. Note s. 3 DAA 2021 child as a victim; personally connected.	'Serious effect', which includes causing the victim to fear violence will be used against them on two or more occasions, and/or causing the victim serious alarm or distress which has a substantial adverse effect on their usual day-to-day activities.	The defendant must know, or ought to know, that the behaviour will have a serious effect on the victim. (subjective or objective)
Scotland *Domestic Abuse (Scotland) Act 2018* (Scot) s 1	Course of behaviour	Abusive (defined in s. 2)	Victim, child under 18, or another person. The defendant and the victim are partners or ex-partners.	Physical or psychological harm, including fear, alarm or distress. Note that it is not a requirement that the harm in fact occurs.	A reasonable person would consider the course of behaviour to be likely to cause the victim to suffer physical and psychological harm, *and* either (i) the defendant intended the behaviour to cause the victim such harm, or (ii) the defendant was reckless as to whether the behaviour would cause the victim such harm. (objective and subjective)

Ireland *Domestic Violence Act 2018* (IR) s 39	Persistently	Controlling or coercive (not defined in statute or guidance)	Victim only. The victim may be the defendant's spouse, civil partner or someone with whom they were or are in an intimate relationship	'Serious effect', which includes causing the victim to fear violence will be used against them or to experience serious alarm or distress that has a substantial adverse impact on their usual day-to-day activities	The defendant must knowingly engage in the behaviour, *and* a reasonable person would consider the behaviour likely to have a serious effect on the victim. (subjective and objective)
Northern Ireland *Domestic Abuse and Civil Proceedings Act* 2021 s 1	Course of behaviour s. 4(4) involves behaviour on at least two occasions	Abusive	Victim only. Personally connected s. 5(2) includes intimates and family whether living together or not	Physical or psychological harm which includes 'fear, alarm and distress' (S. 1(3))	A reasonable person would consider the course of behaviour to be likely to cause the victim to suffer physical and psychological harm, *and* either (i) the defendant intended the behaviour to cause the victim such harm, or (ii) the defendant was reckless as to whether the behaviour would cause the victim such harm. (objective and subjective)

20 *Vanessa Bettinson and Ronagh McQuigg*

the criminal law. Section 77 Serious Crime Act 2015 to some extent rectified this issue by requiring statutory guidance on the offence,[15] and this non-binding document remains as the source of the definition for controlling and coercive behaviour in respect of the offence. The Domestic Abuse Act 2021 was an opportunity to provide legislative detail on the term, but does not do so, instead adding it to the list of behaviours that are abusive. In Ireland, concerns were raised by Women's Aid at the lack of clarity around the term controlling or coercive behaviour used in section 39 Domestic Violence Act 2018, who noted that the new offence had not explicitly stated that it included non-physical conduct (Women's Aid (Ireland) 2017). It is this lack of a legally binding definition that could undermine the political intention in Ireland to send 'a clear and consistent message that non-violent control in an intimate relationship is criminal'.[16] Likewise, section 76 Serious Crime Act offence was intended to capture non-violent patterns of behaviour (Wiener, 2020) although McGorrery and McMahon (2019) found different approaches had been taken when analysing media reports covering section 76 cases. Sometimes, defendants were charged with specific offences for individual incidents of physical or sexual harm, alongside a charge of controlling or coercive behaviour. On other occasions, 'The physical or sexual violence was part of a factual matrix constituting' the prohibited behaviour (p. 964). Such different approaches are concerning as they give rise to potential double punishment, with the same behaviour forming the basis of several charges.

The Northern Irish approach has avoided this pitfall, instead prohibiting 'abusive behaviour' in the same manner as section 1 Domestic Abuse (Scotland) Act. A full definition of abusive behaviour is provided by section 2(2) of the 2021 Act stating that it is directed at the victim and is either violent or threatening. The Scottish version is the same except it adds intimidating to the list (section 2(2)(a) Domestic Abuse (Scotland) Act). The understanding that abusive behaviour towards children can be impactful upon the parent victim is recognised under section 2(2)(c) of the 2021 Act. The violent or threatening behaviour must be to purposefully cause a relevant effect upon the victim or be reasonably expected to do so. The latter would be satisfied where, for instance, the defendant is persistently verbally abusive and demeaning, but claims that they did not intend their behaviour to result in harm.[17] Relevant effects are listed under section 2(3) of the 2021 Act as (a) making B dependent on, or subordinate to, A, (b) isolating B from friends, family members or other sources of social interaction or support, (c) controlling, regulating or monitoring B's day-to-day activities, (d) depriving B of, or restricting B's, freedom of action, and (e) making B feel frightened, humiliated, degraded, punished or intimidated.

The Explanatory and Financial Memorandum stated that the inclusion of the relevant effects that can indicate that behaviour is abusive was 'intended to ensure that, for example, psychological abuse, or controlling or coercive

Criminal Offence of Domestic Abuse in Northern Ireland   21

behaviour that could not currently be prosecuted under existing offences, falls within the definition of abusive behaviour (as well as violent or threatening behaviour)'.[18] During Assembly debates on the Bill, the Justice Minister, Naomi Long, commented that 'The effects of the abusive behaviour set out in the Bill are deliberately broad, recognising that each person's experience will be different'.[19] In line with the Scottish offence, no hierarchy is drawn between sexual and physical violence (s. 2(4)(a) of the 2021 Act) and section 1(3) states that the references to 'psychological harm' include 'fear, alarm and distress'.

The extensive legislative definition of the term 'abusive behaviour' in both the Scottish and Northern Irish jurisdictions helpfully articulates how the abuse can manifest in victims' lives, and as a crime signifies condemnation of that behaviour. It is still possible for incidents of serious sexual or physical offences to be charged alongside the domestic abuse offences, where there is sufficient evidence of the abuse beyond that serious incident. In contrast to Scotland, the Northern Irish legislation goes further, detailing the meaning of behaviour in section 4, helping to outline the ways in which the behaviour can be communicated.

Section 4(2) of the 2021 Act addresses the meaning of 'behaviour' and states that:

Behaviour is behaviour of any kind, including (for example) –

(a) saying or otherwise communicating something as well as doing something,
(b) intentionally failing –

    (i) to do something or
    (ii) to say or otherwise communicate something.

The Explanatory and Financial Memorandum stated that 'This could include, for example, a failure to pass on times and dates of appointments or social occasions, a failure to feed a family pet or a failure to speak to or communicate with an individual'.[20] Section 4(3) explicitly captures economic abuse, a broader behaviour than financial abuse, which features as part of many coercive and controlling relationships (Singh, 2020). The Explanatory and Financial Memorandum clarified that such economic abuse which impairs a person's ability to acquire, use or maintain money or other property (section 4(3)(a)) includes shared property or property belonging to parents, and that property would include pets or other animals whether belonging to the victim or to others.[21] Using others to direct abusive behaviour towards the victim is also included under section 4(3)(b) and is intended, inter alia, to involve using a third party to spy on or report on the victim's activities.[22]

22 *Vanessa Bettinson and Ronagh McQuigg*

Frequency/Time frame

Unlike England and Wales, Scotland and the Republic of Ireland, Northern Ireland has specified in legislation the minimum number of occasions when the prohibited behaviour must occur. According to section 4(1)(a) of the 2021 Act, the defendant must engage in 'a course of behaviour' that 'involves behaviour on at least two occasions (section 4(4))'. Making this condition legally binding should assist the prosecutorial and investigative authorities considerably, and enable cases to be brought at an early opportunity, rather than requiring a victim to endure longer periods of abuse. Whilst not included in statute, the offences in other jurisdictions are also intended to require a pattern of behaviour, described as persistent, repeated or continuous or a course of behaviour, that requires conduct occurring on at least two or more occasions (Bettinson, 2020). The clarity provided in the Northern Irish offence, suggests a confidence in drafting the offence that is afforded by the ability to reflect on the existing models and is to be welcomed as it should engender greater consistency in court decisions.

In building cases, investigators and prosecutors will have to be mindful that cases can only be built from conduct that occurs after the legislative date. The statutory guidance issued by the Department of Justice clarifies that behaviour that predates 21 February 2022 can only be subject to the criminal law applicable at the time it occurred.[23] McGorrery and McMahon (2019) warn that courts in England and Wales have been crossing the line of non-retroactivity in domestic abuse offences that consider a course of conduct. To avoid potential appeals, Northern Irish prosecutors will need to take care when creating the indictment over the time frame that forms the charge under section 1 of the 2021 Act. However, the course of behaviour model now enables narrative to be introduced about the nature of the relationship, and conduct occurring prior to the commencement date of the Act can be admissible and used as part of that narrative. The past can explain the history of the relationship and how it has effected the victim (Bettinson and Robson, 2020).

Harm

Section 3(1) of the 2021 Act asserts that the offence can be committed whether or not the behaviour in question in fact caused harm. This approach mirrors that contained in sections 1(2) and (3) and section 4(1) Domestic Abuse (Scotland) Act 2018. However, for an offence to be committed under section 76 Serious Crime Act 2015, the behaviour must have a 'serious effect' on the victim, and the defendant must know or ought to have known that the behaviour would have such an effect (s. 76(1)). According to section 76(5), the defendant 'ought to know' that which 'a reasonable person in possession of the same information would know'. Under section 76(4), the behaviour in question will be deemed to have had a 'serious effect' if it causes the victim to fear, on at least two occasions, that violence will be used against them, or if it causes the victim serious alarm or distress which has a substantial adverse effect on their normal day-to-day activities. Section 39 of the Republic of Ireland's Domestic Violence Act 2018 uses a broadly similar approach to that of section 76 Serious Crime Act, in that according to section 39(1) of the Irish legislation, for an offence to be committed the defendant must 'knowingly' engage in the relevant behaviour, this behaviour must have 'a serious effect' and it must be established that a reasonable person would consider the behaviour likely to have such an effect. The term 'knowingly' is not however further defined. Under section 39(2), the behaviour will be deemed to have had 'a serious effect' if it causes the victim 'to fear that violence will be used against him or her', or causes the victim 'serious alarm or distress that has a substantial adverse impact on his or her usual day-to-day activities'. Unlike section 76(4) Serious Crime Act, there is no requirement that the victim has feared that violence will be used against them 'on at least two occasions'. The approach adopted by the Northern Irish legislation, as with the Scottish Act, is thus broader than that adopted by section 76 Serious Crime Act and section 39 of the Republic of Ireland's Domestic Violence Act.

Also, under the Northern Irish and Scottish Acts, for an offence to be committed, there is no need to prove that the behaviour in question actually caused harm, but only that the behaviour was likely to cause physical or psychological harm, and that the defendant intended to cause such harm or was reckless as to whether such harm was caused. As the Justice Minister commented during debates in the Assembly on the Northern Irish Bill, this reflects 'the resilience of the victim or that, for many, abusive behaviour has effectively become normalised'.[24] Herring (2020, p. 124) remarks in respect of the Scottish legislation that 'This approach has some benefits as it allows for a prosecution in cases where the victim is unwilling or reluctant to give evidence and so proof of the impact on them is difficult'. As Bishop and Bettinson (2018, pp. 10–12) discuss, the need to prove that serious harm has occurred has caused problems in establishing successful prosecutions under section 76 Serious Crime Act, and so it appears meritorious that this requirement has not been adopted under the Northern Irish legislation.

Relationship

Under section 1(1) of the Northern Irish legislation, for the offence to be committed, the parties must be 'personally connected' to each other. Section 5(2) states that the parties are 'personally connected' if they are, or have been, married to each other or civil partners of each other; they are living together, or have lived together, as if spouses of each other; they are, or have been, otherwise in an intimate personal relationship with each other; or they are members of the same family. According to section 5(3), being 'members of the same family' encompasses B being A's parent, grandparent, child, grandchild, sister or brother. Northern Ireland has purposefully not mirrored section 1 Domestic Abuse (Scotland) Act when it comes to who can be the parties to the offence. The Statutory Guidance on the domestic abuse offence issued by the Northern Ireland Department of Justice notes that in 2020/2021 a significant number of domestic abuse cases involved either a parent and child or other familial relationship.[25] Scotland restricts the section 1(1) Domestic Abuse (Scotland) Act offence to those in an intimate relationship, which reflects the established domestic abuse policy in that jurisdiction. Similarly, the offence of coercive control contained in the Republic of Ireland's Domestic Violence Act must be committed against a 'relevant person' (s. 39(1)), with this phrase being defined as meaning the spouse or civil partner of the defendant or a person who is or was in an intimate relationship with the defendant (s. 39(4)). However, Northern Ireland's policy has been to include wider familial relationships in its definition of domestic abuse.[26] During Assembly debates on the Northern Irish legislation, the Justice Minister commented that 'the devastating impact of familial domestic abuse on victims should not be underestimated and should be captured by this new offence'.[27] The wider framing of domestic abuse relationships has also been adopted by England and Wales. Whilst section 76(1)(b) Serious Crime Act requires parties to be 'personally connected', sections 76(2) and (6) do not reflect an identical meaning to section 5 of the Northern Irish legislation. As Cairns (2017, pp. 265–266) remarks,

> On the one hand, it can be argued that there is a stronger case for narrowness in the interests of capturing effectively the distinct moral wrong of domestic abuse (which has been said to arise from its systematic nature and the abuse of trust involved) and avoiding overcriminalisation. On the other hand, it can be argued that if individuals other than partners or ex-partners are also capable of experiencing systematic abuse that erodes their freedom and has a significant impact on their daily lives, then the offence should be more widely available to ensure that these individuals are not arbitrarily denied legal protection based on relationship status.

In addition, it is noteworthy that the definition of 'personally connected' contained in section 5(2) of the Northern Irish legislation includes those who have lived together as if spouses of each other. Ex-partners are also included under section 1(1) of the Scottish legislation and section 39(4) of the Republic of Ireland's legislation, and section 68 Domestic Abuse Act 2021 has now amended section 76 Serious Crime Act to extend to ex-partners. Respondents to the Department of Justice's 2016 consultation were of the opinion that a domestic abuse offence should encapsulate situations in which ex-partners are continuing to use coercive control even after separation,[28] and it appears that such an approach is to be welcomed. As Cairns (2017, p. 265) comments, 'Research has consistently shown that those in

Criminal Offence of Domestic Abuse in Northern Ireland 25

abusive relationships are at greatest risk of serious abuse when they are trying to leave their partner or when recently separated'.[29] Also, child contact arrangements can provide opportunities for former partners to engage in abuse (Cairns, 2017, p. 265).[30]

Children

Under section 9(1) of the Northern Irish legislation, the offence is aggravated if a relevant child is involved, for instance, if a child witnessed the offence taking place. An equivalent provision is found in section 5 Domestic Abuse (Scotland) Act, however, neither section 39 of the Republic of Ireland's Domestic Violence Act nor section 76 Serious Crime Act encompasses such a provision. The fact that Northern Ireland has chosen to follow the approach of Scotland in this regard is to be welcomed, given the harm that can be caused to children by exposure to domestic abuse (Mills, 2008). As Herring (2019, p. 95) comments, 'There is widespread acceptance that children raised in a household where there is domestic violence suffer in many ways, as compared to households where there is not'. The impact on children of being raised in families in which there is domestic abuse may include 'behavioural, cognitive and emotional problems, leading to depression, anxiety, truancy and low educational achievement . . . interpersonal problems and poor social skills' (Herring, 2019, pp. 95–96). During Northern Ireland Assembly debates on the Bill, the Justice Minister commented that 'We . . . know that witnessing domestic abuse is devastating for children and can have a long-lasting impact on their well-being . . . I consider these provisions essential in recognising the damaging effect that domestic abuse can have on children'.[31] Additionally, under section 8(1), the domestic abuse offence is aggravated if the victim was under the age of 18 at the time when the offence was committed.[32] There is no equivalent provision in the relevant legislation of any of other jurisdictions in the UK and Ireland. The Committee for Justice reported that generally these aggravator clauses were welcomed by the organisations which submitted evidence in relation to the Bill.[33]

However, according to section 11(1) of the Northern Irish legislation, a child under 16 years of age cannot be the direct victim of the domestic abuse offence. This provision is unnecessary in the Irish and Scottish contexts as the offence is restricted to intimate partner relationships. However, an equivalent provision is nevertheless contained in section 76(3) of the Serious Crime Act. According to the statutory guidance to the latter, the rationale for the inclusion of this provision is that abusive behaviour in such circumstances is covered by other aspects of the criminal law relating to child abuse.[34] Likewise, the statutory guidance on the Northern Irish legislation states that such abuse should be dealt with under child protection legislation, including the child cruelty offence found in section 20 Children and Young Person Act (Northern Ireland) 1968.[35]

26 *Vanessa Bettinson and Ronagh McQuigg*

Mens Rea

Criminal offences not only outline the prohibited conduct, they also require a blameworthy state of mind, unless they are an offence of strict liability. The Northern Irish offence of domestic abuse has mirrored the Scottish offence in terms of the state of mind a defendant is required to have when committing the offence. It involves two stages, the first of which is objective, requiring that a reasonable person would consider the course of behaviour to be likely to cause the victim to suffer either physical or psychological harm. On the one hand, this has the benefit of rejecting a defendant's argument that they themselves did not appreciate that their behaviour would cause such harm to the victim. However, the successful implementation of an objective approach will be determinant on the criminal justice decision-makers' understanding of the harm coercive and controlling behaviour can cause. In Scotland, the introduction of the Domestic Abuse (Scotland) Act was accompanied by training for Police Scotland at the expected cost of £825,107 from 2018 to 2020[36] which can go some way to assuaging this concern. Northern Ireland government public awareness initiatives will be important to educate the public about behaviours that have previously not been recognised in law, and to ensure that the reasonable person would appreciate the harm they can cause in the context of domestic abuse. The second stage of the mens rea requirement is a subjective one and covers both the highest level of culpability, those who intended to cause the victim physical or psychological harm; and the lesser degree of blameworthiness, those who are reckless as to causing such harm (s. 1(2)). The breadth of this second limb of the mens rea requirement can be justified as the maximum penalty for the domestic abuse offence, as is the case in Scotland, is 14 years imprisonment. This therefore allows the court to consider the seriousness of the harm and the level of culpability in mitigation during the sentencing hearing. The Northern Irish statutory guidance in a footnote explains that the term recklessness includes situations where the defendant disregards the consequences of the danger, lacks caution or is rash (p. 10). Consequently, this ensures that a defendant who admits their behaviour cannot escape liability on the basis that they claim that it was not their aim or purpose to cause the victim harm, on condition that 'the court is satisfied that the accused's behaviour would cause such harm' (p. 10).

Comparing similar requirements with England, Wales and Ireland, Northern Ireland has taken 'the more considered approach to mens rea for this kind of offence' (Bettinson, 2020, p. 209). Whilst section 76(1)(d) Serious Crime Act adopts a subjective or objective approach in that the accused either knows or ought to have known their conduct would cause harm, the penalty for the offence, limited to five years imprisonment, does not reflect the higher levels of harm and culpability involved. Whereas, the Irish requirement sets a higher threshold for the prosecution to prove having both a subjective and objective element under section 39(1)(c) Domestic Violence Act 2018 and carries a maximum five years imprisonment penalty. The prosecution will fail to establish guilt, if the accused did not knowingly engage in coercive and controlling behaviour. In opting to mirror the Scottish approach to the mens rea requirements, Northern Ireland has avoided the limitations in the English and Welsh, and Irish offence models, offering a greater opportunity to secure a conviction and a sentence that reflects the seriousness of the prohibited behaviour and the harm it causes.

Defence

Under section 12(1) of the Northern Irish legislation, 'it is a defence for A to show that the course of behaviour was reasonable in the particular circumstances'. The Committee for Justice was of the view that 'given the scope of the offence and the wide personal connection, the Clause provides a necessary balance to the Bill'.[37] However, the Committee proceeded to assert that it expected the Department of Justice 'to closely monitor the use of this defence', and that if there is 'any indication that the defence is being manipulated by perpetrators or is providing a "loophole" for abusive behaviour the Department must take swift action to provide a remedy'.[38] The statutory guidance states that this defence constitutes 'an important safeguard to ensure that those acting in the best interests of others are not criminalised', however it is intended that the defence would only be used in very limited circumstances.[39] The statutory guidance suggests that this defence could apply, for example, if an individual has a partner with an alcohol or gambling addiction and for that reason prevents them from associating with certain people or having control of the household finances.[40] In applying the test for prosecution,[41] according to the statutory guidance, prosecutors will look for sufficient evidence to support the commission of an offence, and will then consider whether any defence put forward by the suspect is reasonable. If it is accepted that the defence is reasonable, the evidential test will not be met and it will not then be necessary for prosecutors to look at public interest considerations. If the evidential test is met and the defence is not accepted as being made out, only then will prosecutors apply the public interest test.[42] The guidance also states that 'given that the defence relates to an offence that involves a course of behaviour it will not be enough to simply state that it was a one off'.[43]

A similar defence is contained in section 6 Domestic Abuse (Scotland) Act. A 'reasonableness' defence is also found in section 76(8) Serious Crime Act, although for this defence to be applicable, not only must the behaviour in question be 'in all the circumstances reasonable' but the defendant must demonstrate that he or she was acting in the best interests of the person against whom the behaviour is exerted. In addition, it is stated that this defence cannot be used in relation to behaviour that causes fear of violence (s. 76(10)).

28 *Vanessa Bettinson and Ronagh McQuigg*

No such 'reasonableness' defence is found in section 39 of the Republic of Ireland's Domestic Violence Act.

Penalty

Under section 14 of the Northern Irish legislation, a person who commits the domestic abuse offence is liable, on summary conviction, to imprisonment for a term not exceeding 12 months or a fine (or both); or, on conviction on indictment, to imprisonment for a term not exceeding 14 years or a fine (or both). This is identical to the penalties which may be imposed for committing an offence under section 1 Domestic Abuse (Scotland) Act. By contrast, a person who commits an offence under section 76 Serious Crime Act or section 39 of the Republic of Ireland's Domestic Violence Act is liable on conviction on indictment to a term of imprisonment of only five years.[44] Bishop (2016, p. 72) comments in respect of the section 76 offence that 'As it carries a maximum sentence of only five years imprisonment, there is . . . an inference that it is less serious in nature than direct physical violence'. Bishop (2016, p. 72) remarks that coercive control may cause extreme psychological harm, which can result in victims taking their own lives (Munro and Aitken, 2020), and proceeds to state that 'if coercion and control were viewed along the same lines as the spectrum of criminal offences against the person, arguably at its very peak, it is as serious as an offence of grievous bodily harm with intent and thus should carry the same maximum sentence of life imprisonment'. A number of respondents to the Department of Justice's public consultation of February 2016 stressed 'the need for a strong sentencing regime with the offence, to reflect the seriousness of domestic abuse/coercive and controlling behaviour and the significant adverse impact this type of abuse has on victims'.[45] It is welcome that the Northern Ireland Assembly took note of such responses and chose to follow the approach of the Scottish legislation by adopting a maximum term of imprisonment of 14 years for commission of the new domestic abuse offence. During Assembly debates on the Bill, the Justice Minister remarked that 'It is . . . essential that we set a penalty that corresponds with the seriousness of the offence'.[46] As stated in the Explanatory and Financial Memorandum, 'The nature of the penalties is intended to reflect the cumulative nature of the offence over time, that it may cover both physical and psychological abuse and also the intimate and trusting nature of the relationships involved'.[47]

Conclusion

In conclusion, the creation of a domestic abuse offence for Northern Ireland is an immensely positive development. The introduction of this offence brings Northern Ireland into line with other jurisdictions within the UK and Ireland,

Criminal Offence of Domestic Abuse in Northern Ireland **29**

and also with human rights standards, in terms of criminalising coercive and controlling behaviour. The fact that the very clear deficiency in Northern Ireland's legislative response to domestic abuse has now been addressed is greatly to be welcomed. Although this development was certainly overdue, it is true that being the final jurisdiction within the UK and Ireland to criminalise such behaviour has enabled Northern Ireland's approach to be informed by the earlier legislation enacted in other jurisdictions and, to some degree, has allowed Northern Ireland to 'cherry pick' the most positive aspects of the approaches of these jurisdictions. As the Justice Minister stated during Assembly debates on the Bill, 'Importantly, as part of our deliberations, we . . . considered offences in other jurisdictions relating to controlling and coercive behaviour, including what is often perceived as the Scottish gold standard'.[48] Nevertheless, the experiences of other jurisdictions have demonstrated the issues that arise in relation to the operationalisation of offences of coercive control (Bettinson and Robson, 2020; Bishop and Bettinson, 2018), and it is likely that Northern Ireland's will similarly face challenges in implementing its new domestic abuse offence. These challenges will be further considered in subsequent chapters of this book.

Notes

1 Department of Justice, 'Domestic Abuse Offence and Domestic Violence Disclosure Scheme – A Consultation', 5 February 2016, www.justice-ni.gov.uk/sites/default/files/consultations/doj/consultation-domestic-violence.PDF.
2 BBC News, 'New abuse law "held up by lack of NI Assembly"', 19 January 2018, www.bbc.co.uk/news/uk-northern-ireland-42739589.
3 Department of Justice, op. cit.
4 Domestic Abuse and Family Proceedings Bill, Explanatory and Financial Memorandum, at 1–2.
5 BBC News, 'New abuse law "held up by lack of NI Assembly"', 19 January 2018, www.bbc.co.uk/news/uk-northern-ireland-42739589.
6 Northern Ireland Assembly, 'Official Report: Tuesday 28 April 2020', Naomi Long MLA, Justice Minister.
7 Discussion of this Act can also be found in McQuigg (2021).
8 The Domestic Abuse and Civil Proceedings Act (Northern Ireland) 2021 (Commencement No. 1) Order (Northern Ireland) 2022.
9 Domestic Abuse and Family Proceedings Bill, Explanatory and Financial Memorandum, at 4.
10 Domestic Abuse and Family Proceedings Bill, Explanatory and Financial Memorandum, at 5.
11 Domestic Abuse and Family Proceedings Bill, Explanatory and Financial Memorandum, at 6.
12 Department of Health, Social Services and Public Safety and Department of Justice, 'Stopping Domestic and Sexual Violence and Abuse in Northern Ireland – A Seven Year Strategy', March 2016, www.justice-ni.gov.uk/sites/default/files/publications/doj/stopping-domestic-sexual-violence-ni.pdf, at 2.
13 Scottish Government, Equally Safe – Reforming the Criminal Law to Address Domestic Abuse and Sexual Offences: Analysis of Consultation Responses (2015).

30 *Vanessa Bettinson and Ronagh McQuigg*

14 Department of Justice, 'Domestic Abuse Offence and Domestic Violence Disclosure Scheme – A Consultation, Summary of Responses', 2016, www.justice-ni.gov.uk/sites/default/files/consultations/justice/domestic-abuse-offence-domestic-violence-disclosure-scheme-summary-of-responses.pdf.

15 Home Office, 'Controlling or Coercive Behaviour in an Intimate or Family Relationship – Statutory Guidance Framework', December 2015, https://assets.publishing.service.gov.uk/government/uploads/system/uploads/attachment_data/file/482528/Controlling_or_coercive_behaviour_-_statutory_guidance.pdf.

16 Seanad Eireann debate, 2 May 2018, Deputy Charles Flanagan, Minister for Justice and Equality.

17 Domestic Abuse and Family Proceedings Bill, Explanatory and Financial Memorandum, at 7.

18 Domestic Abuse and Family Proceedings Bill, Explanatory and Financial Memorandum, at 7.

19 Northern Ireland Assembly, 'Official Report: Tuesday 28 April 2020', Naomi Long MLA, Justice Minister.

20 Domestic Abuse and Family Proceedings Bill, Explanatory and Financial Memorandum, at 8.

21 Domestic Abuse and Family Proceedings Bill, Explanatory and Financial Memorandum, at 8.

22 Domestic Abuse and Family Proceedings Bill, Explanatory and Financial Memorandum, at 8.

23 Department of Justice, 'Abusive Behaviour in an intimate or family relationship – Domestic Abuse Offence, Statutory Guidance, Part 1 of the Domestic Abuse and Civil Proceedings Act (Northern Ireland) 2021 and other matters as to criminal law or procedure relating to domestic abuse in Northern Ireland', February 2022, www.justice-ni.gov.uk/publications/abusive-behaviour-intimate-or-family-relationship-domestic-abuse-offence-statutory-guidance, at 24.

24 Northern Ireland Assembly, 'Official Report: Tuesday 28 April 2020', Naomi Long MLA, Justice Minister.

25 Department of Justice (2022), op. cit., at 11.

26 Department of Health, Social Services and Public Safety and Department of Justice, op. cit., at 2.

27 Northern Ireland Assembly, Official Report: 28 April 2020.

28 Domestic Abuse and Family Proceedings Bill, Explanatory and Financial Memorandum, at 2.

29 See also Humphreys and Thiara (2003).

30 See also Barnett (2015).

31 Northern Ireland Assembly, 'Official Report: Tuesday 28 April 2020', Naomi Long MLA, Justice Minister.

32 However, according to section 11(1), A does not commit the domestic abuse offence in relation to B by engaging in behaviour that is abusive of B at a time when B is under the age of 16 and A has responsibility for B.

33 Committee for Justice, Report on the Domestic Abuse and Family Proceedings Bill, Report: NIA 48/17–22, 15 October 2020, at para. 26.

34 Home Office, 'Controlling or Coercive Behaviour in an Intimate or Family Relationship: Statutory Guidance Framework', December 2015, at 6.

35 Department of Justice (2022), op, cit., at 20.

36 www.gov.scot/binaries/content/documents/govscot/publications/foi-eir-release/2021/02/foi-202000106685/documents/foi202000106685-information-released/foi202000106685-information-released/govscot%3Adocument/FOI202000106685%2B-%2BInformation%2Breleased.pdf.

37 Committee for Justice, op. cit., at para. 376.

38 Committee for Justice, op. cit., at para. 378.

Criminal Offence of Domestic Abuse in Northern Ireland 31

39 Department of Justice (2022), op. cit., at 17.
40 Department of Justice (2022), op. cit., at 17.
41 The test for prosecution can be found in Public Prosecution Service, 'Code for Prosecutors', July 2016, www.ppsni.gov.uk/sites/ppsni/files/publications/PPS%20 Code%20for%20Prosecutors.pdf, at 12. For a prosecution to be brought, the evidence which can be presented in court must be sufficient to provide a reasonable prospect of conviction (the evidential test), and prosecution must be required in the public interest (the public interest test).
42 Department of Justice (2022), op. cit., at 17–18.
43 Department of Justice (2022), op. cit., at 18.
44 Serious Crime Act 2015, section 76(11)(a); and Domestic Violence Act, section 39(3)(b).
45 Domestic Abuse and Family Proceedings Bill, Explanatory and Financial Memorandum, at 2.
46 Northern Ireland Assembly, 'Official Report: Tuesday 28 April 2020', Naomi Long MLA, Justice Minister.
47 Domestic Abuse and Family Proceedings Bill, Explanatory and Financial Memorandum, at 11.
48 Northern Ireland Assembly, 'Official Report: Tuesday 28 April 2020', Naomi Long MLA, Justice Minister.

References

Barnett, A. (2015) '"Like Gold Dust These Days": Domestic Violence Fact-Finding Hearings in Child Contact Cases', *Feminist Legal Studies*, 23, pp. 47–78.
Bettinson, V. (2016) 'Criminalising Coercive Control in Domestic Violence Cases: Should Scotland Follow the Path of England and Wales', *Criminal Law Review*, 3, pp. 165–180.
Bettinson, V. (2020) 'A Comparative Evaluation of Offences: Crimialising Abusive Behaviour in England, Wales, Scotland, Ireland and Tasmania', in McMahon, M. and McGorrery, P. (eds.) *Criminalising Coercive Control: Family Violence and the Criminal Law*. Singapore: Springer, pp. 197–217.
Bettinson, V. and Bishop, C. (2015) 'Is the Creation of a Discrete Offence of Coercive Control Necessary to Combat Domestic Violence?', *Northern Ireland Legal Quarterly*, 66, pp. 179–197.
Bettinson, V. and Robson, J. (2020) 'Prosecuting Coercive Control: Reforming Storytelling in the Courtroom', *Criminal Law Review*, 12, pp. 1107–1126.
Bishop, C. (2016) 'Domestic Violence: The Limitations of a Legal Response', in Hilder, S. and Bettinson, V. (eds.) *Domestic Violence – Interdisciplinary Perspectives on Protection, Prevention and Intervention*. London: Palgrave Macmillan, pp. 59–79.
Bishop, C. and Bettinson, V. (2018) 'Evidencing Domestic Violence, Including Behaviour That Falls under the New Offence of "Coercive and Controlling Behaviour"', *International Journal of Evidence and Proof*, 22, pp. 3–29.
Cairns, I. (2017) 'What Counts as "Domestic"? Family Relationships and the Proposed Criminalization of Domestic Abuse in Scotland', *Edinburgh Law Review*, 21, pp. 262–268.
Douglas, H., Tarrant, S. and Tolmie, J. (2021) 'Social Entrapment Evidence: Understanding Its Role in Self-Defence Cases Involving Intimate Partner Violence', *University of New South Wales Law Journal*, 44, pp. 326–356.
Herring, J. (2019) *Law and the Relational Self*. Cambridge: Cambridge University Press.

Herring, J. (2020) *Domestic Abuse and Human Rights*. Cambridge: Intersentia.

Humphreys, C. and Thiara, R.K. (2003) 'Neither Justice Nor Protection: Women's Experiences of Post-Separation Violence', *Journal of Social Welfare and Family Law*, 25, pp. 195–214.

McGorrery, P. and McMahon, M. (2019) 'Criminalising "The Worst" Part: Operationalising the Offence of Coercive Control in England and Wales', *Criminal Law Review*, 11, pp. 957–965.

McQuigg, R.J.A. (2021) 'Northern Ireland New Offence of Domestic Abuse', *Statute Law Review*, early online access: https://doi.org/10.1093/slr/hmab013.

Mills, O. (2008) 'Effects of Domestic Violence on Children', *Family Law*, 38, pp. 165–171.

Munro, V.E. and Aitken, R. (2020) 'From Hoping to Help: Identifying and Responding to Suicidality amongst Victims of Domestic Abuse', *International Review of Victimology*, 26, pp. 29–49.

Singh, S. (2020) 'Economic Abuse and Family Violence across Cultures: Gendering Money and Assets through Coercive Control', in McMahon, M. and McGorrery, P. (eds.) *Criminalising Coercive Control: Family Violence and the Criminal Law*. Singapore: Springer, pp. 51–72.

Stark, E. (2007) *Coercive Control: How Men Trap Women in Personal Life*. New York: Oxford University Press.

Tolmie, J.R. (2018) 'Coercive Control: To Criminalize or Not to Criminalize?', *Criminology and Criminal Justice*, 18, pp. 50–66.

Wiener, C. (2020) 'From Social Construct to Legal Innovation: the Offence of Controlling or Coercive Behaviour in England and Wales', in McMahon, M. and McGorrery, P. (eds.) *Criminalising Coercive Control: Family Violence and the Criminal Law*. Singapore: Springer, pp. 159–175.

Wilson, G. (2017) 'Comparative Legal Scholarship', in McConville, M. and Chui, W.H. (eds.) *Research Methods for Law*. Edinburgh: Edinburgh University Press, pp. 163–179.

Women's Aid (Ireland). (2017) *Women's Aid Submission on the Domestic Violence Bill 2017*. Dublin: Women's Aid.

3 Understanding and Responding to Coercive Control

Lessons Learned From England and Wales

Charlotte Barlow

Since Stark (2007) defined coercive control as a 'liberty crime', much of the contemporary debate surrounding coercive control has been less concerned with whether it is a feature of domestic abuse, as extensive research demonstrates that it is (Schechter, 1982; Stark, 2007), but rather with the extent to which there is a role for the (criminal) law in responding to this kind of abuse.

Over the last decade, introducing a specific offence of coercive control has either been implemented or considered in a number of jurisdictions. For example, specific offences foregrounding coercive control have been introduced in England and Wales, and Scotland; considered in Canada and different states in Australia (Douglas, 2015); and debated in the United States (Tuerkheimer, 2007). In Northern Ireland, a specific offence of domestic abuse was passed into law under section 1 of the Domestic Abuse and Civil Proceedings Act (Northern Ireland) 2021 and this incorporated the criminalisation of coercive and controlling behaviour (Soliman, 2019). Some of these interventions across the globe are gender-specific and some are not; some only apply to intimate partners and others include other family members. However, they all share the view that a new kind of criminal offence is needed to capture the pattern of abusive behaviours embedded in coercive control, that this constitutes a gap in the legal framework and that such an intervention would fill this gap in an innovative way (Wiener, 2020).

This chapter will explore the ways in which the coercive and controlling behaviour offence introduced in England and Wales (section 76, Serious Crime Act 2015) has been responded to by police officers in one police force in England. The chapter compares police officers' perceptions to the lived experiences of victim-survivors, exploring the ways in which opportunities for identifying and understanding the harms of coercive control were often missed by police officers. The implications of these findings are then considered in relation to the Northern Irish context. The chapter concludes with a discussion of the limits of criminalisation approaches in providing safety for women and children, advocating the need for holistic policy responses.

DOI: 10.4324/9781003345305-3

34 *Charlotte Barlow*

Criminalising Coercive Control

The embrace of coercive control in England and Wales was first apparent with its inclusion in the Home Office definition of domestic abuse, introduced in 2013. In 2015, this definition became embedded into legislation, with the introduction of section 76 of the Serious Crime Act, now updated by the Domestic Abuse Act 2021. However, whilst this legislation draws heavily on the work of Evan Stark, there are some notable differences when compared to his work. For example, unlike the legislation introduced in Scotland in 2018, the legislation in England and Wales is gender-neutral and allows for the possibility of other family relationships to be included within its terms (Stark and Hester, 2019; Burman and Brooks-Hay, 2018). The limits of the legislation have been discussed at length elsewhere (Barlow and Walklate, 2022; Walklate and Fitz-Gibbon, 2019). Although Northern Ireland's legislation is also gender-neutral, there are notable differences in the offence in England and Wales. For example, Northern Ireland's legislation has clearer definitions of some key concepts and also refers to 'a course of behaviour that is abusive to another person', similar to the Scottish legislation, rather than coercive and controlling behaviour specifically (McQuigg, 2021). Furthermore, under the Northern Irish and Scottish legislation, for an offence to be committed, there is no need to prove that the behaviour in question actually caused harm to the victim, but simply that the behaviour was likely to cause physical or psychological harm. This again is a significant difference to the England and Wales legislation (McQuigg, 2021; see also Chapter 2 of this volume). However, the main focus of this chapter is how this legislation has been operationalised and understood in policing practice. It is to this context I shall now turn.

Statistics for the year ending March 2019 indicated a fourfold increase in cases of coercive control under section 76 of the Serious Crime Act 2015 receiving a first hearing in a Magistrate's Court, from 309 during the year ending March 2017 to 1177 during the year ending March 2019 (Office for National Statistics, 2019). Given that the police recorded 1.3 million domestic abuse related crimes in the year ending March 2019 and in that same year the Crime Survey for England and Wales estimated that 2.4 million people experienced domestic abuse, these figures highlight the ongoing relatively low usage of the offence. In a detailed statistical and evidenced review of the coercive control legislation in England and Wales (Home Office, 2021), it is pointed out that:

> There is currently a lack of robust data on CCB (coercive and controlling behaviour) prevalence, making it difficult to measure how effective the offence has been at capturing CCB offending. There is no common statistical definition of CCB used across survey data, administrative data

Understanding and Responding to Coercive Control 35

collected by third-sector organisations and research data, making it difficult to compare prevalence and characteristics of CCB across different sources.

In a recent empirical study on the implementation of the 2015 legislation based on Freedom of Information requests from police forces in England and Wales, Brennan and Myhill (2022) found issues with lower charge rates for perpetrators of coercive control offences compared with other domestic abuse offences, and significantly higher rates of evidential difficulties in coercive control cases. Furthermore, whilst McGorrery and McMahon (2021) make some positive claims in this regard, it is important to note that their analysis is based on press coverage of cases. Nevertheless, what has been evidenced is the difficulties associated with translating this law into practice. For example, data reported by the Bureau of Investigative Journalism (2017) illustrated that the initial take-up of this legislation was patchy and suggested varied levels of implementation in different police forces, evidencing issues with 'justice by geography'. Early evaluations also pointed to problems for frontline police officers in 'seeing' coercive control (Wiener, 2017); in practitioner understandings of coercive control more generally (Robinson et al., 2018; Brennan et al., 2018); and problems associated with evidencing this offence (Bishop and Bettinson, 2018). Furthermore, in an ethnographic study of the implementation of coercive control in England and Wales, Myhill et al. (2022) note problematic knowledge and attitudes towards coercive control expressed by many officers, suggesting that systemic and structural change is needed for the potential of the legislation to be realised. In a study analysing police responses to coercive control in partnership with a police force based in the North of England, Barlow et al. (2020) identified that less than 1% of all domestic abuse offences were recorded as coercive control (in the year 2016–2017). This research suggests police officers may be missing key opportunities for identifying such abuse with the tendency to focus on isolated incidents of abuse proving to be persistent.

The focus on physical violence when responding to domestic abuse also influences police officers' assessment of risk and likelihood of arrest in such cases. Tolmie (2018) suggested that the coercive control offence may only lead to successful charges in cases where physical violence is present, consequently minimising the nature of intimate partner violence in non-physical contexts. The empirical work by Barlow et al. (2020) supports this view with many of the (few) successful prosecutions in this research featuring evidence of physical violence. This echoes the earlier findings of Robinson et al. (2018) which pointed to the 'small constellation of risk factors' embraced by police officers in their decision-making in relation to domestic abuse. In sum, issues have been identified with the ways in which this offence has translated to policing practice.

36   *Charlotte Barlow*

Overview of the Study

The data presented here was gathered as part of a British Academy funded study done with the support of Women's Aid (England) and a policing partner in England. This chapter will focus on the data from three data collection phases: a brief overview of relevant quantitative analysis of all (anonymised) recorded crimes of domestic abuse (i.e. crimes marked with a domestic abuse 'flag' on the partner's information management system (IMS) from 1 January 2017 to 1 January 2018); focus groups and semi-structured interviews with police officers; and interviews with victim-survivors of coercive control. Ethical approval was granted by Lancaster University's Faculty of Social Sciences Ethics Committee prior to data collection.

The quantitative, force-level data provided important contextual information for the other phases of data collection. After processing and removal of duplicates, this data showed that there were 5,230 recorded crimes of domestic abuse in this policing area for the calendar year 2017,[1] and 1.8% (93) of cases were recorded as coercive control. This number appears low particularly when compared with other offences (for example, there were 1,447 (27.8%) occasioning actual bodily harm cases over the same time period) though these figures are very much in line with the generally low use of the offence of coercive control for 2017 (Office for National Statistics, 2018). The police force-level data highlights the well-documented gendered nature of coercive control, with 95% of victims of coercive control being women and 93% of perpetrators being men. Coercive control cases were also more likely to occur in an intimate partner context (89%). Comparatively for ABH cases, 79% of victims were women, 83% of perpetrators were men and 80% of cases occurred in an intimate partner context.

Focus groups and semi-structured interviews were conducted with police officers of varying roles and ranks. Recruitment for the focus groups involved an email being sent to all staff, followed by an invitation to a face-to-face briefing session for those who sought further information. Members of staff who wanted to take part contacted the researchers directly via email. A contact in the force facilitated the organisation of the focus groups. Five focus groups with 25 participants in total (22 men and three women) were conducted. Four focus groups were conducted with frontline, investigating officers and call handlers and one with senior members of staff. Two further semi-structured interviews with senior, decision-making officers (both men) were also conducted. Officers were asked questions about their understandings of and responses to coercive control and how they identify coercive control in domestic abuse responses more broadly.

Finally, ten interviews with victims/survivors of domestic abuse/coercive control were conducted. These women were seeking the support of Women's Aid at the time of the interview and Women's Aid supported the research team with the recruitment of participants. This was to ensure that the women were

Understanding and Responding to Coercive Control   37

provided with appropriate support and, if required, counselling after the interviews had taken place. The interviews focused attention on these women's experiences of police responses. The focus group and interview data were coded and analysed using grounded theory and thematic analysis (Braun and Clarke, 2006) to identify overarching themes in the data. In order to enhance inter-rater reliability, two researchers performed this analytic stage where themes were independently identified within the data and then compared and discussed to reach a thematic consensus. Three themes emerged which are of particular relevance to this chapter and the context in Northern Ireland. These are the 'grey area' of coercive control, hostility towards victim-survivors and concerns with a non-victim-centred response. Each of these themes will be discussed in turn.

Coercive Control as a 'Grey Area'

All officers interviewed in the focus groups suggested they faced issues in identifying and responding effectively to coercive control. Some officers explicitly shared their lack of understanding, for example, 'Do I fully understand it? Probably not' (Interview 1) and 'I don't know enough about it, nowhere near as much as I should' (Focus Group (FG)1, Participant (P) 2). The extent of this lack of knowledge experienced by some officers is captured by the following respondent, who had eight years of experience working in the police, including regularly responding to domestic abuse:

> I would probably say I am one out of 10 confident in responding to coercive control. I probably wouldn't even go one to be honest. Even if you speak to a really experienced officer, they don't have a clue either. Guarantee that if you have a detective sergeant on and you ask them about coercive control on your radio, they will probably be sitting at their computer googling coercive control. Because I don't think anyone is confident. No one is comfortable with it and no one knows what it is or isn't.
>
> (FG4, P2)

Whilst some officers suggested that this lack of knowledge provided a possible explanation as to why records for the offence are so low, others suggested it was because coercive control was not a common offence. For example:

> I just think there aren't a lot of coercive control jobs, because there isn't a lot of it out there to be honest.
>
> (FG4, P3)

This assertion contradicts extensive evidence demonstrating that coercive control is common in many cases of intimate partner abuse where there is a male perpetrator and female victim-survivor (Stark, 2007; Barlow and

38   Charlotte Barlow

Walklate, 2022; Hester, 2013). Others suggested that issues with identifying coercive control also extend to the victim-survivors themselves, for example:

> I also think a lot of victims don't understand what the offence is. Usually it's just part of their normal life and they may not realise what they are experiencing is against the law. I remember this one woman I went to, her partner was so controlling of her. Controlled her phone, Facebook, her money, everything. But she just couldn't see it was happening to her until it eventually clicked in her head.
>
> (FG2, P4)

Victim-survivors of coercive control often occupy a false world created by the perpetrator, unable to make their own choices or live their lives autonomously (Barlow and Walklate, 2022). Gas-lighting, isolation and deprivation often prevent women from understanding experiences within their relationship as abusive (Bettinson and Bishop, 2015). Perpetrators will often use specific techniques to coercively control a victim that are unique to that person and relationship, making it difficult for third parties to identify and understand what is going on. This is particularly the case when abusive behaviours within a relationship are viewed in isolation rather than as a wider pattern of abuse. Behaviours may seem trivial to someone outside the relationship when viewed in isolation, but it is often difficult for victims to articulate the magnitude and impact of what is happening to them. The complexities in translating these nuances to policing practice are captured by this senior officer:

> One of the things with coercive control is the grey area- when does something become controlling? What's the difference between me saying to my partner, for instance, I don't want you mixing with that person for this and this reason, or trying to control them? Or are you having the discussion with them because you think x might not be a good person? We just haven't got a grip on that I don't think. It's really complex.
>
> (Interview 1, senior officer)

The value of coercive control as a clinical concept is significant, providing victim-survivors with a meaningful way of understanding their experiences of ongoing strategies of intimidation, isolation and control extending to all areas of their life depriving them of their liberty. However, for coercive control to be effectively translated into law and policy, there need to be clear distinctions between when behaviours become controlling *and* coercive. The complexities and nuances associated with this have been discussed at length elsewhere (Barlow and Walklate, 2022; Kuennen, 2007). Although the Northern Irish legislation has gone some way to address this

Understanding and Responding to Coercive Control **39**

by using the term 'a course of behaviour that is abusive to another person' rather than coercive control, there is still a lack of clarity in relation to the nuances discussed earlier. Furthermore, many victim-survivors may not recognise their relationships as abusive at all if there is no physical violence present, as physical violence is often more readily associated with domestic abuse in comparison to control and psychological abuse (Gill, 2004). Collectively herein lie some of the difficulties in translating this concept into law and criminal justice practice, whereby officers must determine and identify coercive control within relationships when such distinctions are often complex for victim-survivors themselves to identify and when the distinctions between controlling *and* coercive behaviours are often difficult to capture. These issues are particularly pertinent, when situated within the broader context of hostile attitudes towards victim-survivors of domestic abuse.

Hostility Towards Victim-Survivors

Twelve of the police officers in our focus groups displayed varying degrees of hostility towards victim-survivors of domestic abuse beyond the context of coercive control specifically. For some officers, this hostility was focused on those victim-survivors who withdraw/retract their complaint to the police when officers arrive, particularly repeat victims. For example:

> Half the time you're dealing with people and all you get is verbal abuse from both parties by the time you get there . . . 'why do you keep coming here. Let us live our lives' and you almost want [to] say 'yeah! I do want to let you live your life . . . but we've had a call sorry and I've got to do my job'.
>
> (FG4, P3)

> I see so many of the same people, day in day out, repeats, constant repeats. I would be lying if I said I was always fully invested when I go to them. They just don't help themselves and usually by the time we get there they change their tune.
>
> (FG2, P1)

This latter quotation, in particular, highlights the issue with officers viewing repeat victims as problematic or less worthy of resource investment. This issue has been identified elsewhere (Loftus, 2009). However, of significance here is that in spite of the coercive control guidance suggesting that police officers view domestic abuse as an ongoing process, with repeat victimisation arguably providing an example of this, understanding domestic abuse through this lens may not have translated into policing practice in reality.

40   *Charlotte Barlow*

A second way in which this hostility emerged in the focus groups related to the notion of victim-survivors having 'agendas', which was articulated by five officers. This is evidenced in the following quotations:

> Victims have agendas . . . they do. They say things to make themselves look better so it's hard to get the full picture in coercive control cases.
>
> (FG2, P5)

> The thing is with coercive control, I know it will be abused by some women. People say things like 'we're going through a separation, but in our relationship he used to do this and that' and I'm like, ok, first things first, why are you only just reporting this now? Secondly it's often not coercive control even if they think it is. So if for instance you get one where the husband held the finances. You ask 'what, you had no money at all', 'well I had some money . . . ' and when you speak with him he says 'she's crap with money' and it's like, well actually, that's not controlling then is it. Or another one might say 'oh he controls what I wear', but then you look through her Facebook profile . . . You'd never let her out like that! (laughs) you know, 'if that's what you're allowed to wear, I'd hate to think what you're not allowed to wear then!' so it has become sort of overused and misrecognised at times.
>
> (FG5, P2)

For the latter quotation, in particular, there are at least two issues at play. Firstly, this officer is denying victim-survivors' experiences of abuse if they do not fit with his expectations of what a 'true' victim looks like. This highlights the potential for victim hierarchies (Carrabine et al., 2004) to influence the ways in which police officers respond to domestic abuse, with those perceived as being 'worthy' or 'blameless' victims receiving a more supportive response. Secondly, the officer suggests that victim-survivors reporting their experiences of abuse sometime after the event is indicative of them fabricating or exaggerating the extent of the abuse. Victim-survivors do not report their experiences of abuse to the police for many and varied reasons, such as fears of not being believed, fears for their own safety and safety of their children or financial difficulties (Tolmie, 2018). Abuse can also escalate once a relationship has ended (Monckton-Smith, 2021). This therefore captures some of the ways in which the nature of coercive control may not be fully understood by some police officers.

Furthermore, despite there being more domestic abuse laws, guidance and policy than has ever existed before in the UK and across the globe, it appeared that many officers still generally viewed domestic abuse as 'rubbish work'. This is captured by the following quotations:

> I think for some people, I think the word domestic has got a bad name. A lot of people hear the word domestic on their radio and are like 'I don't

Understanding and Responding to Coercive Control 41

want to do that'. It can be uncomfortable, because you are intruding on people's private life.

(FG1, P1)

If there is a burglary, or a violent crime, if that comes in at the same time as coercive control, you know where most of the resources and energy goes.

(FG3, P1)

Collectively, police officers' perceptions of 'blameless victims' and conceptions of domestic abuse being 'rubbish' police work influenced many officers' overall response and the support provided to victim-survivors. This has particular implications for coercive control, given the difficulties police officers face in understanding and identifying this behaviour more broadly (Barlow et al., 2020; Barlow and Walklate, 2021). The Police Service of Northern Ireland has recently released its action plan to tackle violence against women and girls (2022). Included in this action plan are aims centred upon being perpetrator and prevention-focused and taking violence against women and girls seriously. In many ways, this plan is commendable, particularly due to the collaborative way in which it was developed by working with partnership organisations, the voluntary sector and victim-survivors. However, the quotes outlined earlier suggest that more law, guidance, policy or action plans alone are perhaps not enough to shift or change persistent attitudinal issues related to domestic abuse (Hoyle and Sanders, 1998; Loftus, 2009). Furthermore, the underlying negative attitudes towards responding to domestic abuse were also felt by victim-survivors themselves, particularly in relation to coercive control.

Lack of Victim-Centred Responses

All the victim-survivors we spoke with suggested that police officers faced difficulties in effectively responding to coercive control. This particularly centred around their inability to identify coercive control in the frontline response and subsequent investigative stage. For example,

Every time I called it was always considered a 'domestic argument'. It never went beyond that. I never questioned it as I didn't know myself what was happening.

(Victim-Survivor (VS) 2, female,
Pakistani-British)

I just feel like they didn't have a clue. It was never considered for me. Most of the time officers wouldn't spend more than 15 minutes with me. I called on three occasions and it was only the last time, when I felt more able to talk about my experiences and I had an officer that I felt was

42   *Charlotte Barlow*

really listening to me, that I felt able to try to talk about my experiences more.

(VS4, white British, female)

This last quotation in particular suggests that effective responses to coercive control may often be influenced by the individual officer assigned to the case. Police officers typically focus on responding to what is measurable (such as incidents of physical violence or criminal damage) rather than a process of abuse (i.e. coercive control), which I have referred to elsewhere as being 'incidentalism' (Barlow and Walklate, 2021). Responding to domestic abuse cases which do not feature measurable aspects (such as physical violence) when officers turn up on scene therefore contrasts with expectations typically associated with how officers respond to violence and abuse more generally. This is an important consideration when thinking about how coercive control may be operationalised in policing practice in a Northern Ireland context, as these responses do not occur in a vacuum.

Furthermore, victim-survivors also suggested issues with problematic attitudes and responses to domestic abuse displayed by officers more broadly, particularly by frontline officers. Much of this centred around the women we spoke with feeling negatively judged by officers rather than supported. For example:

After one of the times (the police) came out, I made the choice to go back, and one officer explicitly said, 'if you're going to keep going back, what is the point of us supporting you'. I just felt so judged, by his general tone and demeanour. I just shut down then, didn't want to engage as I felt embarrassed.

(VS7, white British, female)

This reinforces the negative attitudes towards victims discussed earlier in the chapter, whereby repeat victims in particular are perceived as being a 'waste of resources' and time. Other examples include:

They would ask me things like 'what did *you* do' or '*you* must have done something to make him feel like that towards you', which made me think I had done something wrong.

(VS5, Black British, female)

Sometimes you can feel judged. You know the police would be like 'where are the kids?' and I would be like they are with me I don't palm by kids off. Then they would like check the house and check there was food in the fridge and I felt like I was being judged as a mum by them. Are you judging how much of a good mother I am and if I feed my kids?

(VS9, white, female)

Understanding and Responding to Coercive Control 43

The quotations here highlight the ways in which victim blaming continues to infiltrate police responses to domestic abuse, which was clearly a significant barrier for the women we spoke with in reporting their experiences to the police or maintaining engagement as their case progressed. Responses to coercive control need to be situated within this broader context of policing domestic abuse, as captured by the following quotation:

> but you know, from my first experience with the police 21 years ago to the most recent time, nothing had changed. So I doubt it's changed now, even if we do have this new offence. A new offence can only do so much, but if the same response happens, it doesn't make a difference. It's not good is it?
>
> (VS3, white British, female)

Collectively, attitudinal issues and victim blaming clearly continue to influence police responses to victim-survivors. The introduction of any new domestic abuse or coercive control legislation therefore needs to be situated within this context. As the victim-survivor quoted earlier indicates, new legislation alone will not eradicate underlying problematic attitudes. These nuances need to be thought through when considering how the new domestic abuse offence will be operationalised in Northern Ireland moving forward.

Implications for Northern Ireland: The Need for Holistic Responses

There is no doubt that the harms associated with coercive control are significant (Stark, 2007), however, there have been notable issues with the implementation of the coercive and controlling behaviour offence in England and Wales. Issues include low use of the offence, low prosecution rates, issues with police officers' understandings of how to respond effectively to coercive control, a lack of victim-survivor-centred responses and broader attitudinal issues related to domestic abuse. These issues should be thought through when implementing similar offences in other jurisdictions. As Northern Ireland has taken a similar approach to criminalisation to England and Wales (i.e. creating a domestic abuse offence which features behaviours constituting coercive control), there are important considerations for this jurisdiction in particular, which will be summarised in turn.

Firstly, when implementing this offence, there needs to be shared understandings and definitions of what constitutes coercive control, including when control becomes *coercive*, by all agencies tasked with supporting victim-survivors. A key issue with police understandings of coercive control evident in the study discussed in this chapter is officers perceiving this form of abuse to be a 'grey area' and often constituting 'one word against the other'. Much of this ambiguity stems from a lack of shared understandings and clear definitions of coercion *and* control. The Northern Irish legislation uses the

44 *Charlotte Barlow*

terminology 'a course of abusive behaviour' to capture the cumulative process of coercive control and a definition of what constitutes 'abusive behaviour' is included. However, there is ambiguity regarding when 'abusive behaviour' amounts to coercive control. Arguably, all relationships involve persuasion and/or influence (Dutton and Goodman, 2005). However, a key feature of a relationship being *coercive* and controlling is the presence of fear, that is, one person (usually a woman) restricts, changes or limits their behaviour in response to a partner's demands because they are afraid of them. Of significance to this discussion is who decides when and what behaviours are coercive and controlling. Victim-survivors should be the key informant, and decades of feminist scholarship has highlighted the importance of listening to women's voices in, for example, recognising women's ability to assess their own levels of risk in the context of intimate partner abuse (Barlow and Walklate, 2021; Barlow et al., 2020). However, the identification of behaviours as coercive in intimate relationships becomes more complex when it is considered whether women recognise their experiences as such. Herein, lie some of the difficulties in translating this concept into law and criminal justice practice, whereby officers must determine and identify coercive control within relationships when such distinctions are often complex for victim-survivors themselves to identify. We see some of these identification issues played out in the quotes from police officers discussed previously, with many officers suggesting that they themselves and often victim-survivors face difficulty in understanding what constitutes coercive control, due to the complex and individualised nature of this type of abusive behaviour.

However, it is also problematic for other people, particularly state representatives, to tell women what they are experiencing is coercive control, especially when their intervention is uninvited. The issues with state interference in women's lives and women's resistance to this are well documented, a particularly pertinent issue for minoritised and marginalised women (Sokoloff and Dupont, 2005; Barlow and Walklate, 2022). State actors, perhaps unintentionally, often fail to appreciate the social and cultural contexts of many women's real lives with law and policy emanating from a monolithic view of lived experience. For some women, although domestic abuse is a significant source of harm in their lives, it is not the only source of harm. State intervention can potentially be seen as more harmful for themselves, their family and their community. Collectively, there are at least three implications for the policing and criminal justice response arising from these issues. Firstly, agencies tasked with responding to coercive control should ensure they have shared understandings and definitions of key terms and concepts. Secondly, the complexities of coercive control and the potential barriers victim-survivors face in articulating these experiences within a criminal justice context need to be carefully and sensitively considered during all interactions with police officers and other criminal justice professionals. Finally, there needs to be a clear understanding that state and criminal justice interventions may not be the preferred solution for all victim-survivors in coercive control cases. Listening to victim-survivors' voices and preferences in how to move a case forward, whether this involves criminal justice intervention or not, should be prioritised.

The second issue relates to the notion of more training or 'rule tightening' often being viewed as a silver bullet to improve police and other agency responses to coercive control. In England and Wales, some police forces have invested substantial funds into rolling out domestic abuse training (which features coercive control). However, despite some improvements, issues with low number of prosecutions for coercive control and relatively low usage of the offence still remain (Brennan and Myhill, 2022). The extent to which training alone can solve the underlying attitudinal problems associated with coercive control is questionable, particularly given the persistent minimisation of domestic abuse in police work (Loftus, 2009) alongside the ever-changing legal framework to which such training and/or education is required to respond. Relatedly calls for improved training are becoming increasingly linked to rule tightening, such as changes to legislation, administrative rules or policy guidelines (Chan, 1997). This approach adopts a mechanistic view of police organisations presuming that changes in practice can be brought about by changes in rules imposed from the top or an external body. The consistent findings by Her Majesty's Inspectorate of Constabulary Reports (HMIC, 2014; HMIC, 2015) pointing to the continuing failures in policing responses to domestic abuse are perhaps illustrative of the folly of such a presumption. Within a Northern Irish context, training may provide 'guidance' to police officers on legal changes and will assist officers' understanding of procedure in responding to coercive control (Waddington, 2012), but it is unlikely to impact on either their understanding of the broader social context and/or the attitudinal changes required in recognising the seriousness of domestic abuse.

Finally, in order to ensure responses to coercive control are victim-survivor centred a whole system, holistic and whole family approach is needed, which extends beyond solely focusing on criminalisation interventions, but rather on expanding the 'web of accountability' (Spencer, 2016). Spencer (2016, p. 277) suggests that:

> A web of accountability comprises various strands including the actions of legal systems (criminal, civil, child protection and family law), service systems and informal networks of victims, families and communities that together hold the perpetrator to account by intervening and monitoring ongoing behaviour.

Adopting holistic responses to coercive control requires much more than multi-agency working, but as discussed previously requires shared understandings and the centring of domestic abuse and its costs in all forms across and between agencies as well as the public more broadly. This kind of holistic

46 *Charlotte Barlow*

vision was proffered by Wilson (1982), and similar approaches have been suggested more recently by Goodmark (2020) and Gribaldo (2021). For Northern Ireland, rather than solely focusing on creating more criminal legislation on domestic abuse (including coercive control), perhaps a bolder vision could be adopted. One such alternative approach could be to follow the lead of the State of Victoria in Australia and demand a Royal Commission on violence against women. The report commissioned in 2016 took a holistic view of domestic abuse (there termed family violence), with the State of Victoria implementing all 227 of its recommendations covering all agencies who may have a role in tackling domestic abuse. Although there have been issues with the longevity in commitments and 'success' of some of these measures, this approach is one such way of doing things differently within the context of domestic abuse. Extensive research highlights the many and varied reasons as to why victim-survivors do not want to engage with the criminal justice system about their experiences of domestic abuse (Tolmie, 2018). Responses to coercive control operating within a wider structural and holistic approach may therefore provide victim-survivors in Northern Ireland with greater opportunities for 'space for action' (Sharp-Jeffs et al., 2018).

Conclusion

In sum, the criminalisation of coercive control in Northern Ireland will undoubtedly benefit some victim-survivors, that is, those who wish to engage with the criminal justice system can articulate their experiences clearly and receive effective support from criminal justice professionals. The criminalisation of this behaviour also sends out a strong public message that this type of abuse will not be tolerated (Bettinson, 2016; Tolmie, 2018). However, as we have seen in England and Wales, there are significant issues with police and other criminal justice agency responses to coercive control, which provide barriers to its successful operationalisation. The victim-survivors we spoke with as part of the study discussed in this chapter felt that their experiences of coercive control had not been effectively responded to by the police and other agencies. These kinds of issues are not unanticipated, as there are historical difficulties in shifting the criminal justice gaze from incidents to processes (Kelly and Westmarland, 2016). Moreover, legislative changes alone cannot lead to improvements in criminal justice responses (Burman and Brooks-Hay, 2018). However, there are opportunities for Northern Ireland to start on a different footing. This includes ensuring shared definitions and understandings of coercive control across all agencies, recognising that training and guidance alone are not 'silver bullets' that will 'solve' any issues with responses to the offence, and developing holistic, whole systems responses that centre the safety and needs of victim-survivors. These suggestions are not easy, but they should be considered to ensure that lessons are learned from the implementation of the coercive control offence in England and Wales.

Note

1 This sample reflects a particular 'snapshot' of police-recorded crime files on the force IMS and each crime file is subject to the principal crime rule. Subsequently, these recorded crimes only represent the most 'serious' crime reported during each occurrence and may be subject to change.

References

Barlow, C., Johnson, J., Walklate, S. and Humphreys, L. (2020) 'Putting Coercive Control into Practice: Problems and Possibilities', *The British Journal of Criminology*, 60, pp. 160–179.

Barlow, C. and Walklate, S. (2022) *Coercive Control*. Abingdon: Routledge.

Barlow, C. and Walklate, S. (2021) 'Gender, Risk Assessment and Coercive Control: Contradictions in Terms?', *The British Journal of Criminology*, 61, pp. 887–904.

Bettinson, V. (2016) 'Criminalising Coercive Control in Domestic Violence Cases: Should Scotland Follow the Path of England and Wales?', *Criminal Law Review*, 3, pp. 165–180.

Bettinson, V. and Bishop, C. (2015) 'Is the Creation of a Discrete Offence of Coercive Control Necessary to Combat Domestic Violence?', *Northern Ireland Legal Quarterly*, 66, pp. 179–197.

Bishop, C. and Bettinson, V. (2018) 'Evidencing Domestic Violence, Including Behaviour That Falls under the New Offence of "Coercive and Controlling Behaviour"', *International Journal of Evidence and Proof*, 22, pp. 3–29.

Braun, V. and Clarke, V. (2006) 'Using Thematic Analysis in Psychology', *Qualitative Research in Psychology*, 3, pp. 77–101.

Brennan, I.R., Burton, V., Gormally, S. and O'Leary, N. (2018) 'Service Provider Difficulties in Operationalizing Coercive Control', *Violence against Women*, 25, pp. 635–653.

Brennan, I. and Myhill, A. (2022) 'Coercive Control: Patterns in Crimes, Arrests and Outcomes for a New Domestic Abuse Offence', *The British Journal of Criminology*, 62, pp. 468–483.

Bureau of Investigative Journalism (2017) 'Questions Raised Over Patchy Take-up of Domestic Violence Law', https://www.thebureauinvestigates.com/stories/2017-11-24/coercive-control-concerns.

Burman, M. and Brooks-Hay, O. (2018) 'Aligning Policy and Law? The Creation of a Domestic Abuse Offence Incorporating Coercive Control', *Criminology and Criminal Justice*, 18, pp. 67–83.

Carrabine, E., Iganski, P., Lee, M., Plummer, K. and South, N. (2004) *Criminology: A Sociological Introduction*. Abingdon: Routledge.

Chan, J. (1997) *Changing Police Culture: Policing in a Multicultural Society*. Cambridge: Cambridge University Press.

Douglas, H. (2015) 'Do We Need a Specific Domestic Violence Offence?', *Melbourne University Law Review*, 39, pp. 434–471.

Dutton, M.A. and Goodman, L.A. (2005) 'Coercion in Intimate Partner Violence; Toward a New Conceptualization', *Sex Roles*, 52, pp. 743–756.

Gill, A. (2004) 'South Asian Women's Experiences of Domestic Violence', *The Howard Journal of Criminal Justice*, 43, pp. 465–483.

48 Charlotte Barlow

Goodmark, L. (2020) 'Reimagining VAWA: Why Criminalization is Failed Policy and What a Non-Carceral VAWA Could Look Like', *Violence Against Women*, 27, pp. 84–101.

Gribaldo, A. (2021) *Unexpected Subjects: Intimate Partner Violence, Testimony and the Law*. Chicago: Hau Books.

Her Majesty's Inspectorate Constabulary (HMIC) (2014) *Everyone's Business: Improving the Police Response to Domestic Abuse*. London: HMIC.

Her Majesty's Inspectorate Constabulary (HMIC) (2015) *Increasingly Everybody's Business*. London: HMIC.

Hester, M. (2013) 'Who Does What to Whom? Gender and Domestic Violence Perpetrators in English Police Records', *European Journal of Criminology*, 10, pp. 623–640.

Home Office (2021) *Review of the Controlling or Coercive Behaviour Offence*. London: Home Office.

Hoyle, C. and Sanders, A. (1998) *Negotiating Domestic Violence*. Oxford: Clarendon Press.

Kelly, L. and Westmarland, N. (2016) 'Naming and Defining "Domestic Violence": Lessons From Research With Violent Men', *Feminist Review*, 112, pp. 113–127.

Kuennen, T.L. (2007) 'Analyzing the Impact of Coercion on Domestic Violence Victims: How Much is Too Much?', *Berkeley Journal of Gender, Law and Justice*, 22, pp. 2–30.

Loftus, B. (2009) *Police Culture in a Changing World*. Oxford: Oxford University Press.

McGorrery, P. and McMahon, M. (2021) 'Prosecuting Controlling or Coercive Behaviour in England and Wales: Media Reports of a Novel Offence', *Criminology and Criminal Justice*, 21, pp. 566–584.

McQuigg, R.J.A. (2021) 'Northern Ireland New Offence of Domestic Abuse', *Statute Law Review*, early online access: https://doi.org/10.1093/slr/hmab013.

Monckton-Smith, J. (2021) *In Control: Dangerous Relationships and How They End in Murder*. London: Bloomsbury.

Myhill, A., Johnson, K., McNeill, A., Critchfield, E. and Westmarland, N. (2022) '"A Genuine One Usually Sticks Out a Mile": Policing Coercive Control in England and Wales', *Policing and Society*, DOI: 10.1080/10439463.2022.2134370.

Office for National Statistics (2018) 'Domestic Abuse in England and Wales', https://www.ons.gov.uk/peoplepopulationandcommunity/crimeandjustice/bulletins/domesticabuseinenglandandwales/yearendingmarch2018.

Office for National Statistics (2019) 'Domestic Abuse in England and Wales', https://www.ons.gov.uk/peoplepopulationandcommunity/crimeandjustice/bulletins/domesticabuseinenglandandwalesoverview/november2019.

Police Service of Northern Ireland (2022) 'Violence against Women and Girls Action Plan', https://www.psni.police.uk/violence-against-women-and-girls-action-plan.

Robinson, A.L., Pinchevsky, G. and Guthrie, J. (2018) 'A Small Constellation: Risk Factors Informing Police Perceptions of Domestic Abuse', *Policing and Society*, 28, pp. 189–204.

Schechter, S. (1982) *Women and Male Violence: The Visions and Struggles of the Battered Women's Movement*. Cambridge, MA: South End Press.

Sharp-Jeffs, N., Kelly, L. and Klein, R. (2018) 'Long Journeys Toward Freedom: The Relationship between Coercive Control and Space for Action-Measurement and Emerging Evidence', *Violence against Women*, 24, pp. 163–185.

Sokoloff, N.J. and Dupont, I. (2005) 'Domestic Violence at the Intersections of Race, Class and Gender: Challenges and Contributions to Understanding Violence against Marginalised Women in Diverse Communities', *Violence against Women*, 11, pp. 38–64.

Soliman, F. (2019) 'The Criminalisation of Coercive Control', *Research and Information Service Research Paper NIAR 103–2019*, Northern Ireland Assembly.

Spencer, P. (2016) 'Strengthening the Web of Accountability: Criminal Courts and Family Violence Offenders', *Alternative Law Journal*, 41, pp. 225–229.

Stark, E. (2007) *Coercive Control: How Men Entrap Women in Personal Life*. Oxford: Oxford University Press.

Stark, E. and Hester, M. (2019) 'Coercive Control: Update and Review', *Violence against Women*, 25, pp. 81–104.

Tolmie, J. (2018) 'Coercive Control: To Criminalize or Not to Criminalize?', *Criminology and Criminal Justice*, 18, pp. 50–66.

Tuerkheimer, D. (2007) 'Renewing the Call to Criminalize Domestic Violence: An Assessment Three Years Later', *George Washington Law Review*, 75, pp. 101–114.

Waddington, T. (2012) 'Cop Culture', in Newburn, T. and Peay, J. (eds.) *Policing: Politics, Culture and Control*. Oxford: Hart, pp. 89–109.

Wiener, C. (2017) 'Seeing What Is "Invisible in Plain Sight": Policing Coercive Control', *The Howard Journal of Crime and Justice*, 56, pp. 500–515.

Wiener, C. (2020) 'From Social Construct to Legal Innovation: The Offence of Controlling or Coercive Behaviour in England and Wales', in McMahon, M. and McGorrery, P. (eds.) *Criminalising Coercive Control: Family Violence and the Criminal Law*. Singapore: Springer, pp. 159–175.

Wilson, E. (1982) *What is to be Done About Violence Against Women?* Harmondsworth: Penguin.

4 The Justice Challenge for Policing Northern Ireland

Training Police Officers in the Law of Control

Rob Ewin

This chapter explores some of the ingredients required for Northern Ireland (NI) policing, and the public, to become engaged in the management of coercive and controlling behaviour in order to protect victims and bring offenders to justice. The identification of controlling behaviours is discussed throughout this book; they stand out as distinguishable from other relationship behaviours. One of the key duties around police work is about the operation of an inquisitive mindset, being evidence-led and victim-motivated, which means that investigators capture the very evidence, and lines of enquiry, which are likely to result in convictions of perpetrators. In order for NI to implement, sustain and pioneer a future-proof policing model, it is critical that alongside established technologies like body-worn video (BWV), and emerging response processes like rapid video response (RVR), the officers are digitally enabled. This means having a fit-for-purpose regime of training and support which is centred around how coercive behaviours work, and how perpetrators may control their victims' lives through technology. Establishing this means officers are easily able to make sense of, and recover, digital evidence without binding these core skills into scarce specialisms. NI police training should demonstrate to officers the distinct behaviours which the evidence base suggests are used by perpetrators (Millar et al., 2021). This includes threats of revengeful sharing of private images, non-fatal strangulation and the manipulation of children. The people of NI have a key role to play in working with policing to ensure that victims are supported, and perpetrators are reported to the authorities for their often cruel, manipulative and now illegal behaviours under the Domestic Abuse and Civil Proceedings Act (Northern Ireland) 2021.

Coercive Control in Northern Ireland – A Priority for the People Becomes a Priority for Policing

Coercive control is a devastating, sometimes carefully disguised, behaviour which impacts on the lives of people all around the globe. Some victims may

DOI: 10.4324/9781003345305-4

never speak of their experiences and may, over time, develop mechanisms to live and cope with their abusers. Victim behaviours should not be used to legitimise inaction by the public or the authorities charged with protecting them. In policing coercive control, responders need to ensure they understand the levels of manipulation which might influence how victims behave during initial reporting. The behaviour might be obviously different to friends and family members, or it might be, as is so often the case, disguised in the compliance of an otherwise heavily controlled victim. There may also be victims who report behaviours to friends, colleagues and their families. These reports might be unavailable to authorities due to the potential fear of antagonising an already intense home environment; this reduces the visibility to authorities of coercive behaviours (Brennan et al., 2019). Evidencing coercive control may then take painstaking time, effort and diligence if the burden of proof is to be clearly established. The wider public also matters to victims. The public need to be alert to what controlling and coercive behaviour is because they may witness some of the often-discreet perpetrator behaviours. Their support is vital to policing responses. This might be around providing victims with safe spaces to report the abuse during normal life, such as visits to shops, appointments for medical treatment and during any period where the victim might be able to signal their need for support. These measures might seem extreme, but research from the periods of the COVID-19 'lockdowns' suggested that isolation made these opportunities to reach out for support more restricted, and in turn, this impacted reporting and amplified perpetrator behaviours (Smyth et al., 2021).

In NI, there is a developing understanding amongst the public as to what coercive control means. A public study, involving 1,292 participants, by Lagdon et al. (2022) indicates that the majority, over 60%, had heard of the term 'coercive control' and knew what it meant; a smaller group, 20%, had heard of coercive control but did not know what it meant; and even less (15%) had never heard of it. This provides an indication of how the wider public might see coercive control, and these understandings matter because although very often coercive behaviours are shielded within private home environments, the behaviours of victims in their normal environments (for example, at work or with other family members) might change. In 2019, the Welsh Government launched a campaign, 'This is Not Love. This is Control'. The campaign's key messages were designed to help the public to distinguish the types of behaviours which are seen in coercive relationships, and there was balanced messaging around victim gender and age. This is vital to the wider acknowledgement of victims being men, women and of various age categories (Bagwell-Gray et al., 2015). Research in New Zealand highlights that establishing effective policing responses to coercive control requires public awareness of the issues to hand (Ali, 2021). The Welsh campaign title is important because many scholars (Fontes, 2015; Kuennen, 2014; Bates, 2020; Clutterbuck, 2019) will distinguish between love and coercive control, whilst many abusers themselves may see love and affection as the very mechanism of binding the victim to continue to be in the relationship with them. The role of statutory bodies like health, policing, fire services and government is to ensure their messaging to the public is clear and originates from research. This is vital in order that public understanding is increased, which may lead to more reports being made to the authorities.

One of the major concerns around coercive control is the impact it has on children, and how children might be used in order to continue the abuse or control of victims post-separation (Katz et al., 2020; Bates, 2019). As public understanding of the behaviours which constitute coercive control is enhanced, it might be expected that those children who have grown into adulthood with experiences of abuse come to share these experiences with others. This may serve to raise awareness to a broader population. It is important to ensure that behaviours which might previously not have been captured by the law are emphasised as now being something that the law and authorities deal with. Callaghan et al. (2018) recognised that children have specific agency when it comes to relationships, but often they are seen as mere bystanders to the abuse, or worse merely 'collateral' damage. In the wider population, the agency of children must be recognised and their experiences given a legitimate acknowledgement in public campaigns. Bagshaw et al. (2011) found that often in abuse cases where there was separation, a child would need to decide how they would approach relationships with the separated parties. This choice can be informed by the parties within the relationship, and also by those more widely available to the child such as educators and friends. This highlights once again the importance of a robust public understanding of the effects of coercive control, and for policing to be effective this should be supported by a broad and clear message across the NI government.

Myhill (2015) emphasised that in order to capture the impacts of abuse, a more comprehensive structure of measures is required to understand where controlling behaviours are reported, and what other behaviours might be present in controlling and coercive relationships. If wider public support is available around controlling and coercive behaviour, then children within the population should be recognised specifically when gathering data about the issue; this may then inform engagement with children at an early and purposeful stage. Lagdon et al. (2022) identified that in NI, 'awareness rates were significantly lower . . . for certain demographic groups; specifically, young people, males, those who are less qualified, and those from a low-income background'. This hints towards a possible starting point for targeted engagement. If a wider, and inclusive, approach is to be achieved, then raising awareness across certain target groups, and acknowledging the specific position of children, is necessary. Soliman (2019) highlighted various approaches to coercive control in England, Scotland, Northern Ireland and the Republic of Ireland, and demonstrated that non-physical abuse (pp. 21–22) accounted for around one-third of domestic abuse cases. This is significant because often

The Justice Challenge for Policing Northern Ireland   53

cases of non-physical abuse are given fewer intensive approaches than cases of physical abuse. These non-physical cases might simply have been labelled 'harassment cases' which may encapsulate some examples of behaviours which could be classed as coercive control. There is then a critical message around how coercive control is different to harassment, and vice versa, how harassment may be a sign of coercive control. In any future analysis of this issue, it will be important to aggregate samples appropriately to ensure these issues are highlighted, especially if they are being discussed with a view to forming policy responses.

Killean (2020) emphasises that the passing of the Domestic Abuse and Civil Proceedings Act (Northern Ireland) Act 2021 is a key starting point for NI's movement on the issue of coercive control. Both Soliman (2019) and Killean recognise that public awareness, and recognition by the courts, are fundamental. However, even before this Act was passed, the NI courts began to recognise some of the behaviours associated with coercive control. In R v O'Neill [2019] NICC 23, the Crown Court, in sentencing the defendant, commented that 'the evidence in this case overwhelmingly points to coercive control' [66], and in A Father v A Mother (In the Matter of UJ and RT) [2021] NIFam 20, the Family Division of the High Court recognised that '[t]he conduct of the father in repeatedly reporting the mother to social services concerning what turn out to be unfounded allegations is, at one level, a form of conscious or sub-conscious attempted coercive control over the mother' [23]. This recognition in the courts, connected with wider public engagement and concern, will move NI towards a journey of making coercive control unacceptable. Killean emphasises that this may assist many victims; there is however a wider public response needed around matters of housing, public health and support for victims and children (Saxton et al., 2020). The 2021 Act does signal an important step towards achieving the wider public acknowledgement that coercive control is a problem for policing and society, for this to be maintained, there should be a wider emphasis on engaging public support and raising awareness of the behaviours which amount to coercive control, and how the impacts on victims might be seen. It is also important for all victim genders to be recognised as potentially legitimate reporters of the types of behaviours which the 2021 Act makes illegal.

The Common-Sense Copper Needs to be Evidence-Led and Victim-Aware

Coercive and controlling behaviour is often not visible; it can form a pattern of behaviours which makes the job of detection by police officers more challenging, and the need for training more acute. Coercive and controlling behaviour became an offence in England and Wales under section 76 of the Serious Crime Act 2015. This provision was a welcome addition to the statute books; Brennan et al. (2021) emphasised that whilst training around the new offence

54 Rob Ewin

had an impact on the number of arrests, the overall number of arrests and convictions remained low. In order for NI to make good progress following its criminalisation of coercive and controlling behaviour, there will need to be a distinct programme of training, not just for officers on the frontline but for all professionals who engage with possible victims. Wiener (2017) highlights that many police practices have evolved around attending reports of domestic abuse, and in some cases, the incident is recorded as 'verbal only domestic no offences disclosed'. This type of response leaves absent any meaningful intervention in the incident, and importantly may leave an offender emboldened to continue the behaviours if there have been no consequences from the act of informing the police. Barlow et al. (2020) emphasise that the response to domestic abuse has to be genuinely holistic, this requires genuine enquiry at the time an incident is reported and more importantly wider efforts to look beyond simply what might be present at the time the police are first called. Also, a successful prosecution strategy must move beyond simply a heavy reliance on the victim's oral testimony (Bishop and Bettinson, 2018). Police training must then move to ensure that officers recognise that some behaviours are more than simply about a verbal argument, but a signal to the authorities that further intervention and exploration as to the possibility of coercive control are required.

Martin (2022) describes the PSNI's training approach to adopting fundamental human rights, drawing attention to the force's sceptics, but also to its distinct approach to moving forward a grounded sense of proving the force's legitimacy in protecting the people of NI. A similar approach might be adopted by the force in the training of its officers around coercive and controlling behaviour. Martin (2022) emphasises the value of building on the 'common-sense copper' – meaning that officers themselves needed to feel that they held a developed common-sense approach to human rights issues before the training was introduced. Police officers themselves identified, where it was possible to do this, not only from their experiences, but also from their training, the job of how human rights operate. The police officers within the study indicated that this formed a fundamental part of the structure of their daily work. It is however highlighted that 'Few officers had positive experiences of police college which was described as too academic and out of touch with practical skills' and that 'The meaning of human rights is constituted through a process of interaction between formal legal norms, organizational cues and police culture but also officers' own values and experiences'. Police training in NI needs to have a legitimate, practical and realistic approach to training on coercive and controlling behaviour. Police training has to be seen as offering a practical solution to officers, not simply addressing the new legislation's legitimacy and rehearsing why it is important. The training must dovetail into the values and experiences of police officers, using examples and case studies which enable officers to think critically about their response to domestic abuse.

The Justice Challenge for Policing Northern Ireland   55

Evidence about the effectiveness of police training can sometimes be limited due to the lack of progress which has been made around evaluating the impact of the training beyond the candidate's satisfaction with the training itself (Davies et al., 2021). There must be a clear link between training and changes to police behaviours in practice to claim full effectiveness. Eigenberg et al. (2012) highlight that there are four major presuppositions around training in domestic abuse. These are (a) there is only one kind of domestic violence; (b) most domestic violence is relatively minor; (c) domestic violence is the same as other crimes and (d) domestic violence calls are extraordinarily dangerous for police officers. Houtsonen (2020) also emphasises that inputs about domestic abuse which are scattered into wider subjects about vulnerability may have the effect of leaving officers to join the dots when it comes to thinking about what constitutes domestic abuse. More importantly, this may make distinguishing coercive and controlling behaviour from other forms of domestic abuse behaviours, a difficult task. In addressing Eigenberg's presuppositions, the training for police officers must carefully balance the possible groups of victims. In practice, this means ensuring that all case studies do not address one type of control, for example, financial; or one type of age category, for example, young people. Millar et al. (2021) emphasise that incidents involving children should be recognised in their own category by training around these scenarios; this is due to the often-unseen impacts that domestic abuse has upon children. However, training should not simply focus on the procedural elements of paperwork. Maple and Kebbell (2021) emphasise that police officers are likely to respond least effectively if the incident they attend demands a significant amount of administration, and the PSNI may need to improve its wider systems to achieve effectiveness.

If, for example, the training is simply focused on the forms officers complete if children are present, then this is unlikely to yield successful application of the training to practice. This is due to the focus on the administration of justice, and not the business of gathering evidence or eliciting further information. In England and Wales, there is some evidence that research forming a 'what works' underpinning to the actions taken by police forces has been accepted by many senior ranks and new officers. This is thanks largely to a persistence in training towards understanding how research can contribute to effective police actions – that is, the training is also evidence-based (Hunter et al., 2019). If policing in NI is going to respond effectively to coercive control then it may first need to establish how its officers respond to domestic abuse, considering them as partners in a momentum of change towards challenging coercive behaviour and understanding how it is different. Where children are involved, the service needs to emphasise, through training, the distinct possibility that the children are at least witness to the behaviours, if not themselves capable of being witnesses in criminal proceedings. Calls about coercive and controlling behaviour are unlikely to place officers in direct conflict situations when compared with other incidents, for example, of public order, but there

56 *Rob Ewin*

are likely to be inherent risks faced in simply leaving a victim without any action being taken and this requires a more inquisitive response.

Recently studies have evidenced the need to explore how behaviours within coercive control should be identified, specifically in training. Bond and Tyrrell (2021) highlight that revengeful sharing of pornographic images can have a significant impact on victims and also their continued ability to maintain new relationships once images have been shared. Behaviour such as this might leave victims fearing that reporting to the police risks their images being further shared by the perpetrator or viewed by the authorities. Such fears might become especially acute if the victim works within a high-profile public organisation or is in a position of trust – for example, teachers, lawyers or indeed police officers as victims themselves. Taylor-Dunn et al. (2021) indicate that victims of stalking behaviours can sometimes be left feeling that the police simply did not acknowledge the seriousness of their reporting, classifying the call as mere harassment. Training approaches in NI are likely to suggest that officers will need to make the mental shift from their understandings of previous laws which may deal with domestic abuse, and those which now relate to coercive and controlling behaviour. Bond and Tyrrell (2021) indicate that survivors' stories are useful, but that there should be a clear focus on how the elements of other laws dovetail into stalking legislation. The same argument could be made around coercive control.

There is also a need to emphasise in training the likely risk of lawfully held firearms being used as a method of control or offering a distinctly increased risk in cases which lead to homicide (Lynch et al., 2021). This may be most acute around episodes of separation, or changes in the personal lives of the victim and perpetrator. The risk might also be heightened by a destabilising event such as a call to the police. These changes, or separation events, when considered in the context of the threat of a live and lawfully held firearm, could amount to a distinctly increased risk of homicide. This is often due to the antecedent of an extended period of psychological control in which a perpetrator exercises control over the victim even if in very subtle ways through the possession and threat of weapons use (Daw et al., 2022). Other forms of physical control, such as non-fatal strangulation, are being recognised as behaviours often frequent in coercive relationships (Stansfield and Williams, 2021). This may present distinct challenges; often there is no obvious physical trauma to be seen, and in order to evidence this type of injury a medical examination might be needed. Revenge porn, firearms and non-fatal strangulation might sound like extreme events, but they are distinctly recognisable in the literature around coercive control and should not be underestimated when approaching training for new or established officers.

Brady et al. (2022) acknowledge that one of the distinct difficulties in many policing approaches is caused by not applying a sufficient level of investigation to reported instances of behaviours which are likely to form part of a wider coercive and controlling relationship. This relationship goes

The Justice Challenge for Policing Northern Ireland   57

hand-in-hand with police leadership strongly recognising coercive control as a priority crime for their officers. McPhee et al. (2022) emphasise that in seeking justice for victims, there first needs to be evidence on which the police might base their decisions. This relies on the investigation having a strong approach to gathering evidence, and not merely dismissing reports because a victim does not wish to provide the police with a formal statement. Whilst evidence-led prosecutions are often heavily desired, they can simply fail to make sufficient progress because of the approach taken during the initial and extended investigation phases. Porter (2019) indicates that the practices in the Crown Prosecution Service have undergone changes which, in part, disable an individual prosecutor's ability to make decisions in cases which might be difficult to prosecute or have a reduced chance of success, in effect this reduces the appetite for prosecuting cases which are complex and are unlikely to be won without a criminal trial. If NI is to make progress with implementing its new domestic abuse offence, then police officers will need to feel that the prosecutions they propose receive due diligence from prosecutors. There is likely to be a joint task of training here to understand the relationship between roles of police evidence gathering and prosecuting. If policing investigators embrace the challenge of bringing cases to prosecute, only to find that the prosecuting body has limited appetite for it, then policing in return is unlikely to push for these cases to be sent for trial. This is particularly acute when looking at evidence-led cases (those without the distinct support of the victim) because often these cases present a greater risk to victims simply because the investigation is inadequate, or too much emphasis is placed on a victim's account at the expense of other material evidence. Police officers may well be asked to pursue all reasonable lines of enquiry, but in the face of a reluctant victim, they might simply be inclined to finalise the case as being one not meriting further action.

Police officers coming into contact with victims of controlling relationships should be aware that, on first contact, the victim may not be likely to be able to rehearse all of the events which have led to the point of contacting the police. If some events are recalled, these might be those considered most prominent by the victim at that time and a comprehensive forensic interviewing approach is needed. This means that alongside training for responders, there needs to be a more specialist focus on key forensically trained interviewing specialist officers. What is also likely to be required in these more complex instances is a pause to the process of evidence gathering, whilst a fully developed strategy on recovering the victim's account can be developed. This requires skilled and properly trained interviewing officers. If a victim declines to be involved in the process of prosecution, then officers will need to examine how, and if, digital evidence could help prove their case. This may mean undertaking a lengthier investigation to reveal further lines of enquiry. The training around these approaches is likely to be available in NI but perhaps only to those considered specialist 'investigators', and what is needed is

58 *Rob Ewin*

a broadly developed skill set including for those who might respond first. This either means a widening of the training approach, or a process by which the case is handled on first report by a specialist team.

Digitally Smart, Evidence-Enabled Policing to Improve Engagement and Investigation

An investigation into the circumstances of coercive and controlling behaviour is likely to involve an examination in digital spaces where the victim and the perpetrator may leave a trail of breadcrumbs about the coercion and control. In order for justice to be effective in these digital spaces, policing needs to fully embrace the technology, and training, which might assist in engaging with victims, with witnesses and with reasonable lines of digital enquiry. This begins at the moment a victim or witness contacts the police, and this is a vital stage for digital evidence which might only be available for a limited time. There are two promising advances in the technology space: rapid response video (RVR) and body-worn video (BWV). There is however a third and more underdeveloped element, and this revolves around digitally capable, and digitally competent, police officers. Firstly, relating to the importance of first contact, a trial using RVR has shown clearly that the approach offers quicker response times and higher victim satisfaction when compared with traditional responses of police officer attendance (Rothwell et al., 2022). These policing approaches may have distinct benefits to cases of controlling behaviours because they could be more discreet. Importantly, in the RVR experiment, there was also a higher arrest rate which gives police officers greater opportunities to speak with victims without the presence of an offender, or whilst an offender is in custody. Importantly, it is necessary at this early point to understand what digital lines of enquiry might be available and how these could be recovered, especially if these lines of enquiry relate to evidence which has a collapsing time frame.

There is a balance to be struck between improved policing responses and victim privacy. Pfitzner et al. (2022) emphasise that police use of BWV has been heralded as a golden ticket to success in cases of domestic abuse. However, police officers should approach the privacy of the victim carefully, especially around matters which may not amount to evidence of the offence being reported but relate, for example, to the relationship with wider family members or unrelated friends. Whatever the initial approach looks like for victims, there must be adequate provisions for recording the first contact because this is often vital evidence to demonstrate to courts, and juries, the emotions of victims and also how an offender may react, see or treat a victim in the presence of officers. Within the RVR trial, there was a careful selection criterion around the type and nature of the call, and the method applied an appropriate screening of calls where an officer was likely to be required immediately. This requires careful policy considerations and planning. The PSNI

The Justice Challenge for Policing Northern Ireland   59

may choose to adopt a policy approach which reflects, and mandates, that BWV or RVR is the approach used in all reported domestic abuse. However, this needs to be fully incorporated alongside a comprehensive digitally aware policing response.

PSNI responses need to be digitally smart, and the response must involve an assessment of the lines of enquiry which might be digitally held but expiring – the so-called collapsing time frames. This often happens amongst social media platforms such as Snapchat, Kik, Slingshot and Wickr Me. Traditionally, police officers have approached digital lines of enquiry by seizing physical devices, but often new platforms are built with enhanced user privacy in mind, and so seizing devices could be of limited value. Where policing needs to focus is on widening frontline digital curiosity and capability, so whilst RVR and BWV have the potential to advance the policing response, there must also be a focus on policing skills which enhance the digital recovery and digital lines of enquiry at the time of the first response. Dodge et al. (2019) touch on one of the central issues in policing around the use, and processing, of digital evidence – the capacity and capability of investigators. Within England and Wales, there has been a considerable move towards the processing of digital evidence as being an inherent policing specialism. Whilst it may be the case that certain investigations require specialist officers, there has emerged a considerable gap in the skills of first responders to be able to recover digital evidence effectively. Harris and Woodlock (2019) emphasise that many cases of coercive control involve digital evidence, and in some cases, the investigation relies so heavily on digital material they describe it as 'digital coercive control'.

Policing in NI will need to rapidly develop its frontline digital skills awareness if it is to effectively tackle what is likely to be an emerging, and distinctly modern, form of domestic abuse and control. Woodlock et al. (2020) conducted research with 546 Australian domestic violence practitioners and examined the way in which perpetrators used technology as part of their abuse tactics. These findings indicated an extensive use of technology for a range of control measures which included surveillance of the victim and control over online friendships. This type of behaviour can have significant impacts on the safety of victims, especially when policing or partner agencies try to interact with the victim over their devices. The use of mobile phone technology is always rapidly developing, and along with this is a developing means of using phone applications to harvest data from other users (Havard and Lefevre, 2020). It is also worthwhile considering how these smartphone applications might interact with smart-home applications such as doorbells, cameras, locks and security systems (Leitão, 2019). These systems might be helpful in making the home safer but when controlled by an abuser, they may also make the home an unsafe prison space.

Todd et al. (2021) examined 41 UK Domestic Homicide Reviews in relation to the role of technology, and cyberstalking, in domestic homicide cases.

60 *Rob Ewin*

The findings indicated that technology played a major role in facilitating behaviours of control, and perpetrator digital footprints were often overlooked in the police investigation with the success of early intervention being determined by the extent of the investigative digital engagement. Despite the significant literature in this field, Thompson and Manning (2021) highlight that the policing capability is lagging behind modern technology and this in turn is affecting public confidence. Barber (2020) also highlights that the Police Service of England and Wales is not equipped to meet the scale and complexity of digital elements within crime investigation. The PSNI needs to ensure that it makes digital policing the day-to-day business of policing and learns the lessons from policing in England and Wales. This means that alongside their BWVs and RVRs, police officers know how to handle digital evidence and can prevent it from being lost from the point of the very first interaction with the police. This means from the outset of the call to the control room, to the officer of first response and also to the specialist who might well receive the investigation later.

Finally, on sexualised abuse through image sharing, Rappert et al. (2022) set out what is required from policing in response to sexual abuse images, detailing the formal and information processes which when produced in the correct format, can become significant and discreet judicial evidence. It is emphasised that whilst justice agencies often strive for linear investigations, such aspirations fail to acknowledge the messy interrelation of expertise and roles that underpin the transformation of digital devices into evidence. One of these interrelations is that the job of digital evidence recovery begins from the moment that the police are made aware that such evidence may exist. Images of sexual abuse may at first appear in isolation but could later form a dossier of evidence on wider control operated through the possession of such images. This may feed into what might be termed as a victim-aware but evidence-led approach – or, to make the point more explicit, it might be termed a digital-evidence-led approach capable of securing vital evidence. NI may choose to adopt the specialist functions of Digital Media Investigators (DMIs) and whilst they play a vital role in the overall policing response, Wilson-Kovacs (2021) highlights that DMIs require a sustained and coordinated effort of support to professionalise and protect their skills which can be supported by digitally capable responders. Once a core investment of digital skills has been established amongst the frontline workforce, and some specialist skill sets supported with technology and training, there should be a clear focus on the type of response in which these skills might be utilised, and this comes from effective screening in control rooms at the first point of victim contact or reporting. Not all reports to the police will require an emergency response and some reports may also originate from third parties, such as health bodies. O'Doherty et al. (2015) emphasise that healthcare settings are an ideal place to screen for intimate partner violence and these settings may also provide policing with an opportunity to capture digital evidence which may otherwise be lost. Barber (2023) also highlights that for many male victims there are distinct possibilities for screening and detection in healthcare settings. Therefore, there is likely to be a role for first responders to be trained in some elements of digital triage and signposting in healthcare settings.

Considerations for the Future

This chapter has highlighted the importance of a whole system of government and policing response to the problem of coercive control. It is important to recognise that the passing of the 2021 Act in NI signals a significant move towards the crime being dealt with more effectively. This should be reinforced with a rigorous system of police training which focuses first on those responding or receiving reports of the behaviours. This is not simply about police officers, but also control room and public-facing staff. The training needs to be led by the accounts of victims and be focused on how to gather evidence on the effects of the behaviour so that the victim's account is supported by a robust evidence package. Being evidence-led and victim-aware is an important recognition to ensure that investigators do not focus all their efforts on the victim's account at the expense of other lines of enquiry which may prove vital to proving the offence. Investigators and responders also need the skills to recognise digital lines of investigation, and this means that alongside technology such as RVR and BWV, there is a comprehensive approach around digital skills within the wider policing workforce. The nature of coercive control means that there could be many forms of verbal, physical and digital manipulation and it is important for policing to base its response around processes which are tested and measured around their effectiveness.

References

Ali, F. (2021) 'Criminalising Coercive Control in New Zealand: The Implications' (Doctoral dissertation, ResearchSpace. Auckland).

Bagshaw, D., Brown, T., Wendt, S., Campbell, A., McInnes, E., Tinning, B., Batagol, B., Sifris, A., Tyson, D., Baker, J. and Arias, P.F. (2011) 'The Effect of Family Violence on Post-Separation Parenting Arrangements: The Experiences and Views of Children and Adults from Families Who Separated Post-1995 and Post-2006', *Family Matters*, 86, pp. 49–61.

Bagwell-Gray, M.E., Messing, J.T. and Baldwin-White, A. (2015) 'Intimate Partner Sexual Violence: A Review of Terms, Definitions, and Prevalence', *Trauma, Violence & Abuse*, 16, pp. 316–335.

Barber, C. (2023) 'Providing the Right Support and Care for Male Victims of Domestic Abuse', *British Journal of Nursing*, 32, pp. 20–28.

Barber, M. (2020) 'The First Report of the Strategic Review on Policing in England and Wales', Police Foundation, www.policingreview.org.uk/wp-content/uploads/phase_1_report_final-1.pdf.

62 Rob Ewin

Barlow, C., Johnson, K., Walklate, S. and Humphreys, L. (2020) 'Putting Coercive Control into Practice: Problems and Possibilities', *The British Journal of Criminology*, 60, pp. 160–179.

Bates, E.A. (2019) '"I Am Still Afraid of Her": Men's Experiences of Post-Separation Abuse', *Partner Abuse*, 10, pp. 336–358.

Bates, E.A. (2020) '"Walking on Egg Shells": A Qualitative Examination of Men's Experiences of Intimate Partner Violence', *Psychology of Men & Masculinities*, 21, pp. 13–24.

Bishop, C. and Bettinson, V. (2018) 'Evidencing Domestic Violence, Including Behaviour That Falls under the New Offence of 'Controlling or Coercive Behaviour', *The International Journal of Evidence & Proof*, 22, pp. 3–29.

Bond, E. and Tyrrell, K. (2021) 'Understanding Revenge Pornography: A National Survey of Police Officers and Staff in England and Wales', *Journal of Interpersonal Violence*, 36, pp. 2166–2181.

Brady, P.Q., Fansher, A.K. and Zedaker, S.B. (2022) 'How Victims of Strangulation Survived: Enhancing the Admissibility of Victim Statements to the Police When Survivors Are Reluctant to Cooperate', *Violence against Women*, 28, pp. 1098–1123.

Brennan, I.R., Burton, V., Gormally, S. and O'Leary, N. (2019) 'Service Provider Difficulties in Operationalizing Coercive Control', *Violence against Women*, 25, pp. 635–653.

Brennan, I., Myhill, A., Tagliaferri, G. and Tapley, J. (2021) 'Policing a New Domestic Abuse Crime: Effects of Force-Wide Training on Arrests for Coercive Control', *Policing and Society*, 31, pp. 1153–1167.

Callaghan, J., Alexander, J., Sixsmith, J. and Chiara Fellin, L. (2018) 'Beyond "Witnessing": Children's Experiences of Coercive Control in Domestic Violence and Abuse', *Journal of Interpersonal Violence*, 33, pp. 1551–1581.

Clutterbuck, D. (2019) 'Violence in Young Adults' Relationships: Coercive Control and Love', (Doctoral dissertation, University of Bristol).

Davies, P., Rowe, M., Brown, D.M. and Biddle, P. (2021) 'Understanding the Status of Evidence in Policing Research: Reflections from a Study of Policing Domestic Abuse', *Policing and Society*, 31, pp. 687–701.

Daw, J., Halliwell, G., Hay, S. and Jacob, S. (2022) '"You Don't Notice It, It's Like Boiling Water": Identifying Psychological Abuse Within Intimate Partner Relationships and How It Develops across a Domestic Homicide Timeline', *Current Psychology*, pp. 1–15.

Dodge, A., Spencer, D., Ricciardelli, R. and Ballucci, D. (2019) '"This Isn't Your Father's Police Force": Digital Evidence in Sexual Assault Investigations', *Australian & New Zealand Journal of Criminology*, 52, pp. 499–515.

Eigenberg, H.M., Kappeler, V.E. and McGuffee, K. (2012) 'Confronting the Complexities of Domestic Violence: A Social Prescription for Rethinking Police Training', *Journal of Police Crisis Negotiations*, 12, pp. 122–145.

Fontes, L.A. (2015) *Invisible Chains: Overcoming Coercive Control in Your Intimate Relationship*. New York: Guilford Publications.

Harris, B.A. and Woodlock, D. (2019) 'Digital Coercive Control: Insights from Two Landmark Domestic Violence Studies', *The British Journal of Criminology*, 59, pp. 530–550.

Havard, T.E. and Lefevre, M. (2020) 'Beyond the Power and Control Wheel: How Abusive Men Manipulate Mobile Phone Technologies to Facilitate Coercive Control', *Journal of Gender-Based Violence*, 4, pp. 223–239.

Houtsonen, J. (2020) 'Policing of Domestic Violence: Strategy, Competence, Training', *European Police Science and Research Bulletin*, 19, p. 135.

Hunter, G., May, T. and Hough, M. (2019) 'Are the Police Embracing Evidence-Informed Practice? A View from England and Wales', *Policing and Society*, 29, pp. 251–265.

Katz, E., Nikupeteri, A. and Laitinen, M. (2020) 'When Coercive Control Continues to Harm Children: Post-Separation Fathering, Stalking and Domestic Violence', *Child Abuse Review*, 29, pp. 310–324.

Killean, R. (2020) '"A Leap Forward"? Critiquing the Criminalisation of Domestic Abuse in Northern Ireland', *Northern Ireland Legal Quarterly*, 71, pp. 595–618.

Kuennen, T.L. (2014) 'Love Matters', *Arizona Law Review*, 56, pp. 977–1015.

Lagdon, S., Jordan, J.A., Devine, P., Tully, M.A., Armour, C. and Shannon, C. (2022) 'Public Understanding of Coercive Control in Northern Ireland', *Journal of Family Violence*, pp. 1–12.

Leitão, R. (2019) 'Anticipating Smart Home Security and Privacy Threats with Survivors of Intimate Partner Abuse', in *Proceedings of the 2019 on Designing Interactive Systems Conference*, pp. 527–539, https://dl.acm.org/doi/proceedings/10.1145/3322276.

Lynch, K.R., Jackson, D.B. and Logan, T.K. (2021) 'Coercive Control, Stalking, and Guns: Modeling Service Professionals' Perceived Risk of Potentially Fatal Intimate Partner Gun Violence', *Journal of Interpersonal Violence*, 36, pp. NP7997–NP8018.

Maple, E. and Kebbell, M. (2021) 'Responding to Domestic and Family Violence: A Qualitative Study on the Changing Perceptions of Frontline Police Officers', *Violence against Women*, 27, pp. 2377–2398.

Martin, R. (2022) 'Righting the Police: How Do Officers Make Sense of Human Rights?', *The British Journal of Criminology*, 62, pp. 551–567.

McPhee, D., Hester, M., Bates, L., Lilley-Walker, S.J. and Patsios, D. (2022) 'Criminal Justice Responses to Domestic Violence and Abuse in England: An Analysis of Case Attrition and Inequalities Using Police Data', *Policing and Society*, 32, pp. 963–980.

Millar, A., Saxton, M., Øverlien, C. and Elliffe, R. (2021) 'Police Officers Do Not Need More Training; But Different Training. Policing Domestic Violence and Abuse Involving Children: A Rapid Review', *Journal of Family Violence*, pp. 1–18.

Myhill, A. (2015) 'Measuring Coercive Control: What Can We Learn from National Population Surveys?', *Violence against Women*, 21, pp. 355–375.

O'Doherty, L., Hegarty, K., Ramsay, J., Davidson, L.L., Feder, G. and Taft, A. (2015) 'Screening Women for Intimate Partner Violence in Healthcare Settings', *Cochrane Database of Systematic Reviews*, 7.

Pfitzner, N., Walklate, S. and McCulloch, J. (2022) 'Body-Worn Cameras: An Effective or Cosmetic Policing Response to Domestic and Family Violence?', *Criminology & Criminal Justice*, DOI: 10.1177/17488958221108478.

Porter, A. (2019) 'Prosecuting Domestic Abuse in England and Wales: Crown Prosecution Service "Working Practice" and New Public Managerialism', *Social & Legal Studies*, 28, pp. 493–516.

Rappert, B., Wilson-Kovacs, D., Wheat, H. and Leonelli, S. (2022) 'Evincing Offence: How Digital Forensics Turns Big Data into Evidence for Policing Sexual Abuse', *Engaging Science, Technology, and Society*, 8, pp. 8–30.

Rothwell, S., McFadzien, K., Strang, H., Hooper, G. and Pughsley, A. (2022) 'Rapid Video Responses (RVR) vs. Face-to-Face Responses by Police Officers to Domestic

64   *Rob Ewin*

Abuse Victims: A Randomised Controlled Trial', *Cambridge Journal of Evidence-Based Policing*, pp. 1–24.

Saxton, M.D., Jaffe, P.G., Dawson, M., Olszowy, L. and Straatman, A.L. (2020) 'Barriers to Police Addressing Risk to Children Exposed to Domestic Violence', *Child Abuse & Neglect*, 106, DOI: 10.1016/j.chiabu.2020.104554.

Smyth, C., Cullen, P., Breckenridge, J., Cortis, N. and Valentine, K. (2021) 'COVID-19 Lockdowns, Intimate Partner Violence and Coercive Control', *Australian Journal of Social Issues*, 56, pp. 359–373.

Soliman, F. (2019) 'The Criminalisation of Coercive Control', Northern Ireland Assembly, Research and Information Research Paper 03/19.

Stansfield, R. and Williams, K.R. (2021) 'Coercive Control between Intimate Partners: An Application to Nonfatal Strangulation', *Journal of Interpersonal Violence*, 36, pp. NP5105–NP5124.

Taylor-Dunn, H., Bowen, E. and Gilchrist, E.A. (2021) 'Reporting Harassment and Stalking to the Police: A Qualitative Study of Victims' Experiences', *Journal of Interpersonal Violence*, 36, pp. NP5965–NP5992.

Thompson, P. and Manning, M. (2021) 'Missed Opportunities in Digital Investigation. In Jahankhani, H., Jamal, A. and Lawson, S. (eds.) *Cybersecurity, Privacy and Freedom Protection in the Connected World*. Cham: Springer, pp. 101–122.

Todd, C., Bryce, J. and Franqueira, V.N. (2021) 'Technology, Cyberstalking and Domestic Homicide: Informing Prevention and Response Strategies', *Policing and Society*, 31, pp. 82–99.

Wiener, C. (2017) 'Seeing What Is "Invisible in Plain Sight": Policing Coercive Control', *The Howard Journal of Crime and Justice*, 56, pp. 500–515.

Wilson-Kovacs, D. (2021) 'Digital Media Investigators: Challenges and Opportunities in the Use of Digital Forensics in Police Investigations in England and Wales', *Policing: An International Journal*, 44, pp. 669–682.

Woodlock, D., McKenzie, M., Western, D. and Harris, B. (2020) 'Technology as a Weapon in Domestic Violence: Responding to Digital Coercive Control', *Australian Social Work*, 73, pp. 368–380.

5 Prosecuting Domestic Abuse in Northern Ireland

The Challenges of the Trial Process

Jeremy Robson

The creation of the offence of domestic abuse in section 1 of the Domestic Abuse and Civil Proceedings Act (Northern Ireland) 2021 (DACPA) is a long overdue step in affording protections for victims of domestic abuse.[1] The creation of an offence punishing abusers for their actions over a prolonged period of time recognises that acts which of themselves are innocuous may amount to a course of conduct which has a significant impact on the welfare of the victim (McGorrery and McMahon, 2019). This marks a move away from a model of criminalisation which focused on individual acts of violence. The mere fact such behaviour has been criminalised will not be a panacea to the challenge of domestic abuse unless the justice system is able to achieve convictions and recognises the challenges of prosecuting coercive control (McQuigg, 2021).

The simple fact that an offence exists does not guarantee a conviction. In order for the policy objectives to be delivered, the procedural rules need to recognise the challenges which flow from the nature of the offence, ensuring that the decision-makers during the process understand and accommodate these issues. The Anglo-American adversarial trial process draws heavily on an expository model of deciding cases, where evidential rules are developed on a case-by-case basis. This means legal systems can be slow to respond to new challenges and understandings without statutory intervention. The new offence of domestic abuse, which has similarities with offences in other jurisdictions of the United Kingdom (see Chapter 2 of this volume), means a new approach to the collection and presentation of offences in court. As has been illustrated in England and Wales, existing rules of evidence do not always comfortably accommodate offences which are committed over a long period of time (Bettinson and Robson, 2020). These problems arise because 'coercion and control' are not seen as part of the 'legal lexicon of storytelling in the courtroom' (Edwards, 2016, p. 879). Whilst the domestic abuse offence in Northern Ireland does not use the phrase 'coercive control' (instead opting to define in section 2 of the DACPA the types of behaviours envisaged), the overall shape of the offence is largely the same as that of controlling or

DOI: 10.4324/9781003345305-5

66 *Jeremy Robson*

coercive behaviour found in section 76 of the Serious Crime Act 2015 which applies in England and Wales. Northern Ireland's domestic abuse offence recognises that behaviours in the course of a close personal relationship can be manipulated by abusers, and it is these behaviours which are criminalised. In this chapter, I will discuss some of the areas where problems may arise and, drawing primarily on the English experience, consider how these difficulties can be resolved to ensure that a case against an accused can be presented fully.

Issues With the Adversarial Trial

Northern Ireland has its own criminal justice system which broadly resembles that of England and Wales and in many areas is governed by statutes which are identically worded. Cases may be tried summarily in the Magistrates' Court or before a jury in the Crown Court. Domestic abuse is a hybrid offence which may be tried in the Magistrates' Court (where the maximum sentence will be 12 months imprisonment) or on indictment in the Crown Court (where the maximum sentence is 14 years). Prosecutions are brought by the Public Prosecution Service for Northern Ireland (PPSNI) who are responsible for making decisions on charge and preparing cases for trial. In order to obtain a conviction, the prosecution must convince the court of the defendant's guilt to the criminal standard; that requires the court to be 'sure'. The primary means by which a party presents evidence in support of its case is through the oral testimony of witnesses who will give evidence on oath and produce exhibits. Decisions on the admissibility of evidence are, in the Crown Court, decided by the judge in the absence of the jury.

The UK has incorporated the European Convention on Human Rights 1953 (ECHR) into domestic legislation by virtue of the Human Rights Act 1998. Article 6 of the ECHR provides specific protections for a defendant in a criminal trial. The rights of prosecution witnesses and victims are not explicitly protected but it is accepted that the prosecution and criminal justice process engages a number of their rights. In R (on the application of B) v DPP [2009] EWHC 106 (Admin), a refusal to prosecute on the basis of the mental instability of the victim was accepted as a breach of Article 3 (the right not to be treated in an inhuman or degrading way) because the state was under a duty to prosecute criminals who degraded their victims. Victims were granted extra protection through the domestic implementation of the EU Victims' Rights Directive of 2012 which was introduced into domestic legislation via the Victim Charter (Justice Act (Northern Ireland) 2015) Order 2015. This Victims' Charter created minimum standards for the treatment of victims in the justice system (Department of Justice, 2019). There are now minimum expectations of the standards which victims can expect of their service providers and an entitlement to services and support for the victims of crime.

The trial process in Northern Ireland is adversarial. The adversarial model of trial with its emphasis on oral cross-examination of witnesses is often cited as being the most effective method of achieving justice. Cross-examination has been described as 'the greatest legal machine ever invented for the discovery of the truth' (Wigmore, 1940). It is however not without critics who note the traumatic impact of the trial process (Ellison and Munro, 2017). Legal systems have sought to mitigate this through a series of reforms aimed at supporting the witness via special measures, ensuring protection of the dignity of the victim (Doak et al., 2021). In England and Wales, judges can play a significant role in ensuring that child and other vulnerable witnesses are able to communicate clearly in the trial, with a body of case law upholding the principle that judges can control cross-examination of vulnerable witnesses, however, no such jurisprudence exists in Northern Ireland (Doak et al., 2021).

Following the high-profile and controversial rape acquittal of four men in 2018, Sir John Gillen was commissioned to review the adequacy of the criminal justice system in Northern Ireland (Gillen, 2019). Whilst the focus of the review was on the handling of serious sexual offences, many of the conclusions of the report are applicable to domestic abuse cases. This is, in part, because sexual offending plays a role in many instances of domestic abuse and the familial nature of abuse was often cited by victims of sexual violence as being a reason for withdrawing support for prosecutions. It is also, in part, because the systemic deficiencies identified in the justice system are likely to apply regardless of the crime. One particular weakness identified by the review was a lack of coordinated training within the justice system. In particular, Gillen noted there was a continuing lack of understanding about the impact of trauma upon a victim. As I shall discuss later, many of the tools within the laws of evidence which may help facilitate the introduction of evidence require a nuanced judicial interpretation and understanding and if this is lacking they may not be fully deployed.

Securing the Testimony of the Victim

Securing a conviction for domestic abuse requires the prosecution to establish that a series of individual acts took place within the context of an often private relationship. Unlike the English and Welsh legislation, there is no requirement under the Northern Irish legislation to prove physical and psychological harm as an essential element of the offence; it suffices that the behaviour would be likely to cause such harm, and that the accused intended such harm or was reckless as to whether such harm would be caused. This difference is designed to overcome the difficulties which have been encountered in proving harm in England and Wales and creating a 'conduct' offence rather than a 'result' offence. Notwithstanding this difference, it is likely to assist in proving the case if the prosecution can establish that such harm has in fact been caused, and if it has it will make a material difference to sentence; being able to describe and prove the harm caused remains an important part of the case-building process. It is frequently the case that the victim is the sole witness to the behaviour

68   *Jeremy Robson*

and the sole person who can speak of the impact of incidents, and without that testimony the case may fail. Statistically, victim non-participation plays a significant role in the failure of prosecutions. In England and Wales, data from 2022 indicates that 51.4% of domestic abuse incidents reported to the police were not charged as the victim did not support prosecution (Office for National Statistics, 2022). Of those cases which were charged, 23.6% failed to produce a conviction. Of those non-conviction cases, 49.6% of cases were dropped as a result of complainant issues. The indication is that the equivalent figure for other offending is approximately 10% (Crown Prosecution Service, 2011). The reasons for this are numerous and in part relate to the unwillingness of the victim to be exposed to public scrutiny of their lifestyle, intimate relationships and decision-making (Bishop and Bettinson, 2018). Victims of domestic abuse will already have been shamed and humiliated by the perpetrator and the trial process is likely to repeat this process. It is also difficult to discuss the behaviour conducted by the perpetrator when it involves activities which are, on the face of it, not recognisably criminal as the prospects of success may be perceived as low; this is particularly true where the tactics used are non-physical. Many of these factors are similar to those recognised in the Gillen Review as being factors which cause victims to withdraw their support for prosecutions of serious sexual offences. Other factors identified by the Gillen Review include fear of intrusive cross-examination and delays in bringing the case to conclusion (Gillen, 2019).

The justice system can address some of these concerns. The issue of delay is primarily a matter of resourcing and can be alleviated through the provision of courtrooms, judiciary and prosecutors. In 2021, the average time for a case involving a sexual offence to be completed in Northern Ireland was 583 days (The Irish News, 2021). A domestic abuse case is likely to have the same level of complexity and so, it can be assumed, would experience similar delays. Whilst undoubtedly the COVID pandemic extended this waiting list, delays to the justice system were in evidence before 2020 (Northern Ireland Audit Office, 2018). It has been suggested that this backlog may not be cleared until 2028 with the situation being exacerbated by the current absence of an executive (BBC, 2022). Ensuring the availability of courts, judges and prosecutors will allow cases to progress with greater speed through the system which is a vital part of an effective criminal justice policy. Delay is not simply an inconvenience. It impacts upon the memory of the witnesses which, as shall be discussed later, can impact upon the outcome of the trial. It means that survivors are unable to move on with their lives, impacting upon the control the perpetrator exerts. In other cases, some victims may seek to maintain the relationship and will be pressured to withdraw support. In cases where victims do end the relationship, there may still be control post-separation through childcare arrangements and surveillance. The involvement of the criminal justice system creates a structural bond to the abuser beyond her control and this limits her autonomy in negotiating other facets of her life.

The fear that a victim may have of seeing her abuser in court can be partially mitigated through special measures which are designed to provide a degree of protection to a victim from the accused in court and to improve the quality of the evidence, as provided under the Criminal Evidence (Northern Ireland) Order 1999. Special measures may include screening of the witness from the defendant, removal of wigs and gowns, the giving of evidence via video link, and playing of a pre-recorded examination in chief. One provision which appears in the statute but is not yet in practice is video-recorded cross-examination. This enables the witness to have their cross-examination recorded in advance at an early stage in the proceedings to avoid having to attend the trial. The equivalent provision to this is now being used in England and Wales following a successful pilot, however, it is currently restricted to child witnesses and witnesses who are vulnerable as a result of a disability. The pilot noted that the experiences of witnesses were more positive and there was a reduced delay between reporting the offence and being questioned about it (Baverstock, 2016). Consideration could be given to the wider roll-out of this provision as a means of ensuring that the evidence of a victim is challenged appropriately and fairly at an earlier stage in the proceedings and that this evidence can be captured and presented at court.

Special measures can be a helpful tool for the prosecutor seeking to provide assurances to a victim of crime. Most victims of domestic abuse will be eligible for special measures under section 5 of the 1999 Order on the basis they are in 'fear or distress' about testifying. Section 5 of the 1999 Order was amended by section 23 of DACPA to provide victims of domestic abuse offences with automatic eligibility to special measures. This approach (also adopted in relation to victims of modern slavery and sexual offences) enables assurances to be given from the outset of the investigation that special measures will be available in the trial.

In circumstances where the victim does not attend court, the prosecution can consider compelling the witness to attend through the use of a summons. If the witness fails to attend, the witness is in contempt of court. This is a potentially complex area, both legally and ethically. If the parties are not married, then the victim is compellable. If the parties are married, the spouse is only compellable if the offence falls under Article 3 of the Criminal Evidence (Northern Ireland) Order 1999, namely where the offence involves an assault on, or injury or a threat of injury to, the spouse or civil partner or a child or is a sexual offence committed towards a child. In relation to the offence as framed in England and Wales, it has previously been noted that the lack of explicit reference to the types of behaviour potentially creates an ambiguity which could result in it being argued that a married witness is not compellable under the equivalent provision in section 80 of the Police and Criminal Evidence Act 1980 (Bettinson and Robson, 2020). The clearer framing of the meaning of abusive behaviour in Northern Ireland avoids this difficulty.

70 *Jeremy Robson*

The Public Prosecution Service in Northern Ireland sets out its position via its Policy for Prosecuting Domestic Violence in Northern Ireland which states, 'under current legislation we can require a husband or wife to give evidence about an assault or threat of injury. We can also compel unmarried partners or family members to give evidence' (Public Prosecution Service, 2006, p. 17). The Gillen Review notes that 'Training has been delivered to all prosecutors with regard to domestic abuse and additional guidance provided with regard to the decision to summons a witness and, should they fail to attend, seek an arrest warrant' (Gillen, 2019, p. 101).

The fact that compelling the witness is an option does not mean that it is a desirable or appropriate strategy. As Edwards rightly observed, the use of contempt powers to punish a victim who withdraws due to fear is perverse (Edwards, 2012, p. 30). It should therefore not be the central means which is deployed when dealing with a victim who withdraws support. Whilst mandated victim participation has formed part of prosecutorial policy in England and Wales (Hall, 2009), it was designed to be treated as a strategy of last resort. Despite this, there was evidence that this approach was routinely used until 2014, when a change in strategy led to a change of approach (Porter, 2019). Mandating victim attendance has been argued to be a revictimisation of the victim, substituting the state for the abuser (Hanna, 1996). It is also a tactically unwise strategy as it has been noted that a 'compelled but hostile complainant is at best an uncertain proposition for the prosecution' (Ellison, 2002, p. 848).

An alternative to reliance on the testimony of the victim is the 'evidence-led' or 'victimless' prosecution, where the police and prosecuting authorities build a case which does not rely on the testimony of the victim but uses other evidence to prove the case against the defendant. This approach is widely used in a number of jurisdictions and has the advantage of reducing any possibility of the defendant being able to manipulate or intimidate the victim (Ellison, 2002). Gillen notes that there has been a greater use of this (alongside witness summons) in Northern Ireland. The Crown Prosecution Service in England and Wales has adopted this approach and explicitly advises pursuing lines of enquiry which do not rely solely on the victim (Crown Prosecution Service, 2022). Statutory Guidance produced by the Department of Justice in February 2022 provides a list of areas which the police should investigate (Department of Justice, 2022). An agreed checklist with the National Council of Police provides guidance on evidence which might be looked for, including, for example, data-mining software which has been used to track the victim's online behaviour. A subsequent examination of police and prosecutorial practice in this area established that although there was a good understanding of the importance of evidence-led prosecutions, there was limited training and sharing of good practice (CJJI, 2020). Evidence-led prosecutions are a crucial strategy in overcoming the challenges of victim withdrawal and hostility and robust training in this style of case-building is essential for the success of a domestic abuse strategy.

Prosecuting Domestic Abuse in Northern Ireland 71

Whilst developing a robust case is important to any prosecution, not every case will succeed without the support of the victim. This is especially so when the prosecution is relying on psychological harm to prove the offence; whilst the physical injuries from an assault can often be documented through medical evidence and can be clearly linked to a physical act, this is more challenging with psychological harm which is linked to a course of conduct and the narrative of the witness is often necessary to explain the behaviour and its consequences. Whilst there is no requirement for proof of harm, in establishing that behaviour is abusive, the prosecution can seek to establish that the behaviour was directed at causing a relevant effect in section 2(3) of the DACPA. The relevant effects are framed around the consequences on the victim. In certain cases, the nature of the behaviour will be such that the purpose can be clearly established. In other cases, the consequences of the behaviour can only be understood in the context of the dynamics of the relationship which requires a narrative from the victim. If prosecutions are to succeed in these circumstances without the attendance of the victim at court, then prosecutors need to look to introducing the testimony of the victim as hearsay.

Hearsay is admissible in Northern Ireland under Articles 18–22 of the Criminal Justice (Evidence) (Northern Ireland) Order 2004. These provisions mirror the wording of sections 114–118 of the Criminal Justice Act 2003 in England and Wales and so authorities from this jurisdiction provide helpful guidance on how they can be deployed to assist prosecutions in Northern Ireland.

These hearsay provisions were introduced with the express intention of allowing judges' discretion to introduce evidence which was cogent but would otherwise be classified as hearsay (Law Commission, 1997). The gateways for the admissibility of hearsay potentially allow the admissibility of hearsay in a number of circumstances which are helpful in the prosecution of domestic abuse. Article 20 of the 2004 Order allows hearsay evidence to be rendered admissible if the witness is absent for one of a number of prescribed reasons (death (Article 20(a)), illness (Article 20(b)), being overseas (Article 20(c)), being unable to be traced (Article 20(d)) and fear (Article 20(e))). If a party establishes that one of these criteria is met, the evidence becomes admissible subject to a judicial discretion to exclude it. The rationale for this rule is that these circumstances provide an insurmountable barrier outside the control of the parties which justifies an exception to the normal rule that witnesses should give evidence in person. These rules may apply in individual cases but do not provide a universally applicable framework.

It is gateways (b) and (e) that are potentially of the most widespread application, however, both of these are problematic as the factor which makes the evidence admissible may flow directly from the facts of the offence. Under gateway (b), if the illness which prevents the witness from testifying is unrelated to the harm which has been suffered, then no difficulty arises and the focus of the court will be on the cogency of the evidence. If, however, the

72   *Jeremy Robson*

illness is a result of psychological harm which flows from the abuse, then a court is more likely to be cautious in deciding that the gateway is established, especially if there is a factual dispute about the nature of what has happened. Over-reliance on this provision also risks medicalising the harm sustained which, it has been argued, grounds the pathology of an illness in the survivor at the expense of individual agency (James, 2021).

Gateway (e) would seem to offer a broader remedy for the situation where a victim does not give evidence through 'fear'. Unlike the other gateways in this article which simply require proof of the precondition for the criteria to be met, admissibility under this gateway has an additional criterion of requiring judicial leave, involving consideration being given to criteria in Article 20(4). 'Fear', for the purposes of the legislation is to be construed widely and can include financial harm. The UK Supreme Court has confirmed that there is no need for there to be a link between the fear and the accused (R v Horncastle [2009] UKSC 14), however conversely, the Court of Appeal in England and Wales has suggested that the fear must stem from something beyond the facts of the offence itself (R v Boulton [2007] EWCA Crim 942).

In Boulton, the victim had suffered a campaign of physical and sexual assault from the appellant. Having subsequently been intimidated, she did not attend court and the judge allowed her evidence to be admitted. The Court of Appeal dismissed an appeal on the basis that the subsequent intimidation was the cause of the fear and the underlying offences provided a background against which the offence could be considered. They seem however to have accepted the argument that if the only facts which gave rise to the fear were the underlying offences, this would not be sufficient. If this proposition is correct, it proves particularly challenging for offences which capture the entirety of a relationship. Fear and threats of reprisals are often central to the behaviour which is intended to coerce or control the victim and it will be an impossible task to separate them.

A further problem arises in the use of the word 'fear'. The intention of the Law Commission was that this should be considered from the perspective of the victim with the intention of distinguishing between 'fear' and reluctance. Whilst this distinction is necessary, it again grounds the focus upon the victim and her experiences and repeats the power dynamic between abuser and abused. An application to introduce evidence at a trial (which may be several years after an incident has taken place) will require a witness to prove that she remains in a state of 'fear' and will have to align to that criterion. A victim may be in fear of being in the presence of her abuser but may not wish to define her identity in that way, however if she fails to do so, the application will fail.

If this difficulty can be overcome, the court must go on to consider whether or not leave should be granted in the interests of justice. This is an exercise in judicial discretion and as a result is difficult to challenge. The criteria for leave are drafted broadly requiring the court to consider fairness to both parties. Judicial perceptions of fairness are often constructed from their own

Prosecuting Domestic Abuse in Northern Ireland 73

experiences of the constituent parts of a fair trial (Robson, 2022) and without an understanding of factors which justify the admission of the evidence, the risk of non-admission is high.

In circumstances where evidence is not admissible under Article 20, the Court can go on to consider other routes to admissibility. Article 22 of the Order retains the common law exception to hearsay that statements made by a speaker so emotionally overpowered by the event that the possibility of concoction can be disregarded are admissible for the truth of their contents (the 'res gestae' exception). This provision replicates section 118 of the Criminal Justice Act. With the advent of body-worn cameras and recordings of calls to the emergency service, there is often direct evidence which captures the context in which the statement was made. In England and Wales, this provision has been a valuable tool in the prosecution of domestic abuse, enabling the prosecution to introduce evidence of an initial complaint without the maker of the statement testifying. That is not to say its use should be approached uncritically. Barlow records victim-survivors whose evidence has been captured on body-worn cameras as expressing concerns about the need to present in a stereotypical way and the undue focus on the visible facts as they are at the time of interview at the expense of the historic invisible facts (Barlow, 2023).

Res gestae was historically a difficult exception for parties to rely upon requiring an immediacy between the event described and the action. More recent authorities have redefined this principle to include situations where the surrounding evidence is such that the risk of fabrication can be eliminated. The Court of Appeal in Northern Ireland has shown a willingness to use this provision to admit body camera footage when a victim no longer wished to support the prosecution of her attacker (McGuinness v Public Prosecution Service for Northern Ireland [2017] NICA 30). In McGuinness, the Court of Appeal upheld the decision of the trial judge to admit complaints of assault captured on a body camera approximately 20 minutes after an assault. The Court of Appeal accepted that immediacy was no longer a requirement if there was other evidence which allowed the possibility of concoction to be discounted. The court did note (drawing on the approach found in a number of authorities from England and Wales) that it was not appropriate to use this provision to secure a procedural advantage or to prevent cross-examination. Any admission of hearsay under Article 20 is still subject to an assessment of whether it is in the interests of justice to do so. In making this assessment, the trial judge refers to the checklist in Article 16 to assess the cogency of the evidence. It is significant to note that the judge at first instance, in assessing the interests of justice, took into account the public interest as being a factor which was relevant to the determination. The Court of Appeal observed in relation to seeking to use res gestae in these circumstances that

this is an instance of providing support to the complainant in the changed circumstances brought about by the reconciliation of the parties while at

74   *Jeremy Robson*

the same time seeking to deal with the alleged previous conduct of the appellant. This is a balance which the prosecution has to make in deciding whether and in what manner to prosecute the appellant and does not involve any improper motive or device or unfair tactics.

This recognition is helpful to prosecutors and contributes to providing confidence that in exercising judicial discretion, there is some understanding of the importance of proceeding in the absence of the victim.

The res gestae principle, whilst a valuable mechanism for introducing accounts made in the aftermath of discrete offences of violence, offers little assistance to courts dealing with victims who are providing a longer historical account. Whilst there may be an initial incident of violence which initiates the report to the police, historical events which lack any degree of nexus in time to the complaint will not fall within the scope of res gestae and this gateway offers no solution.

The final option which is available for the admissibility of hearsay is the so-called 'safety valve' under Article 18. This permits a judge to admit evidence when it is in the interests of justice to do so, taking into account the factors set out in the provision. In applying Article 18, the court must have particular regard to Article 6 of the ECHR, in particular the right to examine witnesses. The jurisprudence from Strasbourg suggests that the primary focus of this analysis is cogency of the evidence and the reason for the non-attendance of the witness (Spencer, 2014). The European Court of Human Rights has found there to be no breach of Article 6 when corroborated body camera footage was admitted against a defendant (Asch v Austria (1991) 2 Hum. Rts. Case Dig. 67). The fact that failure to prosecute a defendant would amount to a breach of a victim's rights to private and family life is something which can be taken into account (Doorson v Netherlands (1996) 22 E.H.R.R. 330). Application of the criteria under Article 18 is a matter of individual judicial discretion. Whilst McGuiness illustrates that some of the judiciaries are alert to the public interest in ensuring evidence is heard in domestic abuse cases, nothing in Article 18 guarantees judges will all take this approach and the fact that a witness has voluntarily not attended in circumstances which fall short of 'fear' may result in the evidence not being admitted.

The current combination of hearsay rules can be seen as offering a means by which the statement of a victim can be introduced if she no longer supports the prosecution, however, they do not do so in a coherent and consistent way. The broad principle that hearsay evidence may be admissible without interfering with a defendant's right to a fair trial is accepted, however, there is no consistency as to the circumstances which trigger this and it is over-reliant on judicial discretion. States have an obligation to put in place effective law enforcement machinery for the prevention of domestic abuse which would breach an individual's rights to freedom from torture or inhuman or degrading treatment (Article 3) (Opuz v Turkey [2009] ECHR 870). A court system which has no consistent approach to how probative evidence is admitted risks failing to meet this obligation. If the justification for the specific statutory exceptions to hearsay under Article 18 of the Order is that they represent circumstances outside the control of the parties justifying a departure from the normal rule of oral testimony, then there is a compelling argument for an additional gateway which permits the introduction of documentary witness testimony when the witness is a victim of domestic abuse testifying against her abuser. By recognising this as a specific statutory gateway, there is a consistent and objective basis for the admission of evidence which recognises the distinct victimology of cases of domestic abuse.

The addition of this as a criterion to Article 20 would enable courts to start from the point that the reason a domestic abuse victim does not attend is due to the impact of the behaviour upon her and the challenge of testifying about personal and intimate relationships. It would however not allow evidence to be admitted without any challenge or judicial scrutiny. The Supreme Court in Horncastle accepted that the codified regime for hearsay did not interfere with a defendant's right to a fair trial under Article 6 of the ECHR. It noted that the rules were a carefully crafted code which required judicial leave and careful scrutiny of the evidence before it was admitted. It also enabled the defendant to call evidence which undermined the hearsay evidence and required a careful direction to be given to the jury about the risks of convicting on the basis of hearsay evidence. The subsequent decision of the Court of Appeal in R v Riat [2012] EWCA 1509) (which has been followed in Northern Ireland) confirmed that the simple act of proving a gateway was insufficient for evidence to be admitted; the judge had to consider by looking at a checklist of factors set out in section 114 of the Criminal Justice Act (Article 18 of the Order) whether the evidence should be excluded. Only if the court was satisfied that the evidence was sufficiently cogent would it be admitted. Recognising non-attendance as a facet of domestic abuse over which the prosecution has no control would avoid unnecessary argument about the definition of 'fear' and would focus the exercise of discretion on the cogency of the evidence. The outcome of the trial would no longer be centred around the attendance or non-attendance of the witness but would be determined by the quality of the evidence. This would aid decision-making for both the prosecution and defence. It is important to note in any discussion around hearsay that the oral testimony of a witness is often more persuasive than the reading of a statement and that where a victim is able to give evidence this should be the best option.

Historic Abuse and Bad Character

One of the central challenges is that prior to the commencement of the relevant provisions of the DACPA in February 2022 (under The Domestic Abuse and Civil Proceedings Act (Northern Ireland) 2021 (Commencement No. 1) Order (Northern Ireland) 2022), the acts in question were not illegal and the

76 *Jeremy Robson*

defendant is protected from prosecution by the principle against retroactivity. This is potentially an obstacle to capturing the full range of offending behaviour in the early years of the offence (McGorrery and McMahon, 2019). The requirement of a 'course of behaviour' under section 1 requires at least two separate incidents to be committed after the commencement of the Act. If this cannot be proved because the evidence does or may fall outside the period in which the behaviour was criminalised, the prosecution will fail, notwithstanding the severity of the offending.

In other cases, there may be sufficient evidence post February 2022 for the offence to be made out (the acts can occur in a short time frame), however, there will be other evidence of conduct prior to February 2022 which will assist the prosecution in establishing ongoing behaviour or explaining why subsequent behaviour had the impact that it did. If the prosecution wishes to rely upon this evidence (and often it will be impossible not to), consideration needs to be given to how it fits into the relevant bad character provisions of the 2004 Order. As with hearsay, the language of the 2004 Order replicates the language in England and Wales. The most satisfactory approach is to treat this evidence as 'having to do with the facts of the offence' (Article 6) which means it is not classified as bad character and does not need the permission of the court to introduce it. The Court of Appeal in England and Wales has accepted this approach as being appropriate (R v Dandpat [2020] EWCA Crim 244) and there seems no reason why a different approach should be taken in Northern Ireland. In presenting this evidence, it must be made clear to the jury that the evidence does not form part of the case itself and that they must be sure that the offending behaviour took place after the commencement of the offence.

Dispelling Myths

Perhaps the most significant step that needs to be taken in ensuring that allegations of domestic abuse are treated properly is to ensure that there is an understanding of the nature of domestic abuse; both how it is committed and the impact it has on its victims. Concern has been expressed that juries are unable to recognise it in 'all but its grossest form' (Edwards, 2016, p. 882). Where witnesses do give evidence, juries will often be required to assess the credibility of both parties and be satisfied that the account given by the victim is truthful. The process of oral evidence gives primacy to the oral testimony on the day of the trial. Previous statements which are inconsistent with this account are often presented as a means of demonstrating that a witness has been inconsistent and therefore is unworthy of belief.

When a witness gives evidence in a domestic abuse case, they may be narrating a historical account which encompasses a number of years and hundreds of events. Human errors of memory are inevitable over time. When the witness has been subject to repeated traumatic incidents of the type which occur in domestic abuse, research shows that victims of repeated events were more likely to struggle to be able to particularise individual incidents (Dilevski et al., 2020). Myths still exist that the human memory is a 'video camera' and any account which shows inconsistency is likely to be untrue (Simons and Chabris, 2011) and the risk exists that truthful testimony will be discounted as unreliable (Roberts, 2019).

This is not going to be the only myth that risks contaminating the decision-making process. Myths about domestic abuse have long been recognised, including the particularly prevalent misunderstanding that a victim of domestic abuse would leave their abuser (Ewing and Aubrey, 1987). In reality, domestic abuse involves the manipulation of the societal norms which exist in relationships to produce outcomes which are a departure from the norm; without understanding the ways in which this offence operates, there is a risk the offence will be misunderstood.

Addressing myths is something that the criminal justice system has had to address in the context of sexual offending. The Gillen Review noted a number of other myths which had been established in the research which are likely to be applicable to domestic abuse cases; including that false allegations were common, victims made complaints for compensation (which in the case of interpersonal relationships could include advantage in financial and childcare arrangements) and that any form of abuse will leave an injury.

In order to dispel 'rape myths', the judiciaries in Northern Ireland follow the practice of giving directions in their address to the jury drawn from the Crown Court compendium in England and Wales (Judicial College, 2021). The 14 exemplar rape directions address topics such as demeanour and inconsistency and ensure that juries can assess the evidence fairly without being unduly swayed by irrelevant factors. As has been noted, juries 'need assistance to assess the uncommon situations where their common sense does not help them' (Gerry and Sjolin, 2011). Gillen recommended that the impact of such a direction could be improved by addressing these issues at the beginning of the trial, ideally with using a specially prepared video for standardisation. Gillen also recognised that rape myths amongst jurors were, in reality, reflections of rape myths in the public at large and that for them to be effectively eradicated would involve a concerted strategy of public education.

Almost all the recommendations that Gillen makes about addressing myths in sexual offending can be transferred to cases of domestic abuse and require not only shifts in legal practice but also in societal understanding. The introduction of jury directions to dispel myths regarding domestic abuse in England and Wales has been argued for (Bettinson and Robson, 2020) and has received the support of members of the judiciary (Nott, 2022). This would act as an important first step in focusing the minds of the jury on the real issues in the case and removing societal prejudices from the trial process.

78 *Jeremy Robson*

Conclusion

The delivery of a successful strategy to tackle abuse against women and girls must be centred around understanding the lived experiences of victims. The creation of an offence of domestic abuse is the beginning of this process, but it is only through robust and effective prosecution that its aims will be delivered. It is important to recognise that the crime of domestic abuse is in many respects fundamentally different in its nature to the types of offences which the courts have experience in dealing with. In certain aspects, the experience the justice system has developed in supporting victims of sexual violence provides foundations which can be built upon, however, any strategy for effective prosecution will require a rethinking of the approaches to collecting, presenting and analysing evidence. All of this can be achieved whilst maintaining the right of an accused to a fair trial. For any approach to succeed, it must also respect and restore the autonomy and dignity of the victim which will have been eroded during the abuse which has formed the basis of the offence.

The evidence of the victim will always be important, but investigators building cases must be thorough in identifying material which evidences the behaviour independently. This will often involve amassing digital evidence from mobile phones and computers as well as looking for other material which evidences control such as financial records. The more of this material which is available, the lower the risk that the outcome of the trial will be centred in an assessment of the credibility of the victim.

Whilst an understanding of the trial process is essential, there also needs to be a recognition that the criminal justice system sits within a wider societal context and therefore any prejudices or misnomers which find their way into the trial process are in part products of a wider problem. Developing an understanding of these issues in both practitioners and the wider population is desirable not just in terms of criminal prosecutions but in reducing the prevalence of offending behaviour.

Finally, it should be noted that all of these objectives can only be achieved through proper funding. Delays in cases progressing through the justice system result in victims withdrawing their support. Failure to resource training for practitioners and judges results in a system which does not meet the needs of victims and failure to resource investigations fails to ensure that prosecutors can present the strongest case at court.

Note

1 The word 'victim' can be considered problematic in this context and carries with it a sense of disempowerment. Its usage within wider legal and policy contexts carries a specific meaning as one who has experienced the harm of a criminalised act, and carries specific protections, and so for this reason, I shall use it for this chapter.

References

Barlow, C. (2023) '"How Can You Capture What is Hidden?" Police Body-Worn Cameras and Coercive Control', *Journal of Gender-Based Violence*, 7, pp. 163–177.

Baverstock, J. (2016) *Process Evaluation of a Pre-Recorded Cross-Examination Pilot*. Ministry of Justice.

BBC (2022) *NI Courts Backlog 'May Not Be Cleared until 2028', Says minister*, 3 August 2022, www.bbc.co.uk/news/uk-northern-ireland-62054242.

Bettinson, V. and Robson, J. (2020) 'Prosecuting Coercive Control: Reforming Storytelling in the Courtroom', *Criminal Law Review*, 12, pp. 1107–1126.

Bishop, C. and Bettinson, V. (2018) 'Evidencing Domestic Violence, Including Behaviour That Falls under the New Offence of "Coercive and Controlling Behaviour"', *International Journal of Evidence and Proof*, 22, pp. 3–29.

CJJI (2020) *Evidence Led Domestic Abuse Prosecutions*, www.justiceinspectorates. gov.uk/cjji/wp-content/uploads/sites/2/2020/01/Joint-Inspection-Evidence-Led-Domestic-Abuse-Jan19-rpt.pdf.

Crown Prosecution Service (2011) *Violence against Women and Girls Crime Report 2010–2011*. London: Crown Prosecution Service.

Crown Prosecution Service (2022) *Domestic Abuse Legal Advice*, www.cps.gov.uk/legal-guidance/domestic-abuse.

Department of Justice (2019) *Victim's Charter*, chrome-extension://efaidnbmnnnibpcajpcglclefindmkaj/www.justice-ni.gov.uk/sites/default/files/publications/doj/victim-charter.pdf.

Department of Justice (2022) *Abusive Behaviour in an Intimate or Family Relationship – Domestic Abuse Offence, Statutory Guidance, Part 1 of the Domestic Abuse and Civil Proceedings Act (Northern Ireland) 2021 and Other Matters as to Criminal Law or Procedure Relating to Domestic Abuse in Northern Ireland*, www.justice-ni.gov.uk/publications/abusive-behaviour-intimate-or-family-relationship-domestic-abuse-offence-statutory-guidance.

Dilevski, N., Paterson, H.M. and van Golde, C. (2020) 'Investigating the Effect of Emotional Stress on Adult Memory for Single and Repeated Events', *Psychology, Public Policy, and Law*, 26, pp. 425–441.

Doak, J., Jackson, J., Saunders, C., Wright, D., Gomez Farinas, B. and Durdiyeva, S. (2021) *Cross-Examination in Criminal Trials Towards a Revolution in Best Practice?* Nottingham: Nottingham Trent University.

Edwards, S. (2012) 'The Duplicity of Protection - Prosecuting Frightened Victims: An Act of Gender Based Violence', *Journal of Criminal Law*, 76, pp. 29–52.

Edwards, S. (2016) 'Coercion and Compulsion – Reimagining Crimes and Defences', *Criminal Law Review*, 12, pp. 876–899.

Ellison, L. (2002) 'Prosecuting Domestic Violence without Victim Participation', *Modern Law Review*, 65, pp. 834–858.

Ellison, L. and Munro, V. (2017) 'Taking Trauma Seriously: Critical Reflections on the Criminal Justice Process', *International Journal of Eliison and Proof*, 21, pp. 183–208.

Ewing, C. and Aubrey, M. (1987) 'Battered Woman and Public Opinion: Some Realities about the Myths', *Journal of Family Violence*, 2, pp. 257–264.

Gerry, F. and Sjolin, C. (2011) 'Rape Trauma Direction', *Counsel*, https://www.counselmagazine.co.uk/articles/rape-trauma-direction.

80 *Jeremy Robson*

Gillen, S.J. (2019) *Report into the Law and Procedures in Serious Sexual Offences in Northern Ireland*. Belfast: Department of Justice.

Hall, M. (2009) *Victims of Crime: Policy and Practice in Criminal Justice*. Abingdon: Routledge.

Hanna, C. (1996) 'No Right to Choose: Mandated Participation in Domestic Violence Prosecutions', *Harvard Law Review*, 109, pp. 1849–1910.

The Irish News (2021) *Bleak Picture of Log-Jammed Criminal Courts as Northern Ireland's Justice System Sees Longest Delays Ever Recorded*, 10 September 2021, www.irishnews.com/news/northernirelandnews/2021/09/10/news/bleak-picture-of-log-jammed-criminal-courts-as-northern-ireland-s-justice-system-sees-longest-delays-ever-recorded-2442837/#:~:text=Northern%20Ireland%20news-,Bleak%20picture%20of%20log%2D.

James, S. (2021) 'Demedicalizing the Aftermath of Sexual Assault: Toward a Radical Humanistic Approach', *Journal of Humanistic Psychology*, 61, pp. 939–961.

Judicial College (2021) *The Crown Court Compendium (Vol 1)*, www.judiciary.uk/wp-content/uploads/2021/08/Crown-Court-Compendium-Part-I.pdf.

Law Commission (1997) *Evidence in Criminal Proceedings: Hearsay and Related Topics*. London: HMSO.

McGorrery, P. and McMahon, M. (2019) 'Criminalising "The Worst" Part: Operationalising the Offence of Coercive Control in England and Wales', *Criminal Law Review*, 11, pp. 957–965.

McQuigg, R.J.A. (2021) 'Northern Ireland New Offence of Domestic Abuse', *Statute Law Review*, early online access: https://doi.org/10.1093/slr/hmab013.

Northern Ireland Audit Office (2018) *Speeding up Justice: Avoiable Delay in the Criminal Justice System*, chrome-extension://efaidnbmnnnibpcajpcglclefindmkaj/www.niauditoffice.gov.uk/files/niauditoffice/media-files/Speeding%20up%20Justice.pdf.

Nott, E. (2022) 'Addressing Domestic Abuse before, during and after the COVID-19 Pandemic: A Perspective from within the Criminal Justice System of England and Wales', *Criminal Law Review*, pp. 525–544.

Office for National Statistics (2022) 'Domestic Abuse in England and Wales', https://www.ons.gov.uk/peoplepopulationandcommunity/crimeandjustice/bulletins/domesticabuseinenglandandwalesoverview/november2022.

Porter, A. (2019) 'Prosecuting Domestic Abuse in England and Wales: Crown Prosecution Service "Working Practice" and New Public Managerialism', *Social & Legal Studies*, 28, pp. 493–516.

Public Prosecution Service (2006) *Policy for Prosecuting Domestic Violence in Northern Ireland*, www.ppsni.gov.uk/sites/ppsni/files/publications/PPS%20Domestic%20Violencee%20Policy.pdf.

Roberts, A. (2019) 'The Frailties of Human Memory and the Accused's Right to Accurate Procedures', *Criminal Law Review*, pp. 912–933.

Robson, J. (2022) *The Judge as Bricoleur: Bricolage in Decision-Making in Criminal Trials*. In prep.

Simons, D. and Chabris, C. (2011) 'What People Believe about How Memory Works: A Representative Survey of the U.S. Population', *PLoS ONE*, 6.

Spencer, J. (2014) *Evidence of Hearsay in Criminal Proceedings*. London: Bloomsbury.

Wigmore, J. (1940) *Evidence in Trials at Common Law*. Boston: Little, Brown & Company.

6 What Might 'Successful' Coercive Control Prosecutions Look Like?

Antonia Porter

Criminalising Coercive Control

Using the criminal law as a central means of redressing the harms suffered by abused women could be considered limited and myopic (Tuerkheimer, 2003, p. 962; Walklate et al., 2018, p. 127; Douglas, 2008; Goodmark, 2009). Yet, despite those who have expressed reservations about whether 'more law is the answer' (Walklate et al., 2018), engaging in coercive or controlling behaviour towards a person with whom you are personally connected became a criminal offence in England and Wales in 2015.[1] The 2021 Northern Irish offence,[2] just as the English and Welsh one, aims to address the prior disconnect that existed between the experience of living with an abuser on the one hand and abuse as it was being pursued in the criminal courts on the other. Intending to plug a lacuna in the law (Home Office, 2015; Wiener, 2020, p. 159), the coercive control offences in both jurisdictions acknowledge the physical and also the psychological harms – the pervasive fear, the victim's loss of autonomy and her entrapment within the relationship – that had hitherto not been captured by existing criminal offences.

Since the English and Welsh offence was introduced in 2015, the numbers of coercive or controlling behaviour cases reported and prosecuted have increased markedly. In the year ending March 2017, only 4,246 such offences were recorded by the police but that number rose to 33,954 in the year ending 2021 (ONS, 2021), reflecting, undoubtedly, not only the impact of the pandemic on both the prevalence and the intensity of the behaviour but also promulgation and growing awareness of the offence. Greater recognition of the offence is still needed amongst the general public (Home Office, 2021), the police (Barlow, 2019) and criminal justice professionals (Crossman and Hardesty, 2018). Indeed, prevalence rates from the Crime Survey of England and Wales indicate that only a fraction of all coercive control comes to the attention of police or is recorded as such (Home Office, 2021, 1.2). As for report-to-charge conversion rates, following the first six months of the offence, the CPS charged a mere 62 offences. Most recent figures from the year ending 2019 show a rise to 1,112 prosecutions (ONS, 2021). Prosecutors in Northern Ireland may initially therefore expect a mirroring of these low numbers

DOI: 10.4324/9781003345305-6

82 *Antonia Porter*

coming through the system because the offence will be unfamiliar and also due to its non-retrospective nature. However, the ongoing paltry figures in England and Wales also reflect, as this chapter explores, the particular challenges of prosecuting this offence.

Overwhelmingly, defendants in England and Wales convicted of coercive or controlling behaviour have been male.[3] For that reason, coercive control sits as part of the CPS Violence Against Women and Girls Strategy which recognises that such offences are 'committed primarily, but not exclusively by men against women within a context of power and control' (CPS, 2017). The CPS VAWG strategy accordingly aims to improve the prosecution rates, to support victims and to bring perpetrators to justice (CPS, 2016). The Public Prosecution Service in Northern Ireland does not have a strategy specifically dedicated to addressing gender-based violence, though the PPS express the view that they take domestic abuse 'extremely seriously' (PPS, 2022). It follows that as part of such commitments, successful convictions will be paramount and it is to that aim that the chapter speaks. Yet, at the same time, there will be instances when a conviction does not represent the best outcome for the victim-survivor or serve her best interests. So, as part of prosecutors' ongoing duty to review cases on evidential or public interest grounds, when a woman expresses her withdrawal from the prosecution, prosecutors will need to carefully weigh up whether exercising their discretion to discontinue the case is merited. For, even where evidential and procedural challenges can be overcome, if achieving a conviction does not carry clear advantages for the victim-survivor, prosecutors might relinquish institutional expectations to pursue the case to finality. 'Effective' implementation of the new law must therefore proceed with that caveat in mind.

Unique and novel barriers exist to prosecuting coercive control and prosecutors will need to identify and anticipate problem areas. First, the chapter assists prosecutors in understanding the new offence with reference to the work of Evan Stark. Ordinarily, prosecutors will approach criminal transgressions with a reductive focus on the facts of the incident. This chapter, however, invites prosecutors to consider the offence in its fullest context. Yet such an expansive instinct as to the facts is likely to jar with prosecutors' increasingly managerial role and quest for efficiency (Hodgson, 2020, p. 142). As part of this 'opening up' to the context of the offence, prosecutors are encouraged to consider the part they can play in reorienting the criminal justice system to the victim's experience. Second, the chapter considers pre-charge matters such as meeting ongoing disclosure obligations and selecting charge dates that capture the extent of the offence without overloading the triers of fact. And finally, the chapter turns to the contested hearing; assuring prosecuting advocates that loosening the reins when the victim gives evidence in chief may pay dividends and that being expert in the range of tactics and manipulations pursued by perpetrators will assist in the clear presentation and preparation of the case, particularly during speeches.

From 'Violent Incident' to Narrating Context

Criminal offences typically focus attention on a single one-off incident or a number of discrete and identifiable transgressions. The trial itself then comprises an evidential enquiry into the isolated event 'without reference to or a contextualisation of the . . . history' (Rollinson, 2000, pp. 108–109). Witnesses are often told, whilst giving evidence, to answer the question put and not to digress into irrelevant satellite concerns, particularly when a witness threatens to disclose another's past 'bad character' without leave of the court.[4] As such, courts hear only part of victims' stories and their account – taken out of context – 'may resemble something other than the truth' (Tolmie, 2018, p. 52). In the context of domestic abuse, the transactional nature of the criminal offence has typically been reflected in date and time stamped charges under, inter alia, the offences against the person regime.

Stark has called the criminal law's equation of *abuse* with incident-specific *assault* the 'violent incident model' and explains that such a focus infers that the severity of abuse can be calculated by assessment of the degree of injury inflicted or threatened during the spotlighted episode of violence (2012, p. 200). Yet, of course, the 'violent incident model' ignores the *non-violent harms* that may be inflicted by the perpetrator in the course of a controlling and coercive dynamic and it was precisely this gap in the law that the 2015 offence endeavoured to address (Wiener, 2020, p. 165; Barlow and Walklate, 2022, p. 11).

The criminal trial's focus on the identifiable act(s) or violent episode(s) reflects an understanding of domestic abuse that parallels Johnson's 'situational couple violence' typology or what Madden-Dempsey has called 'domestic violence in its weak sense' (Johnson, 2010, pp. 11–12; Dempsey, 2009, p. 126). Both these models describe the so-called 'one off' incidents of violence sparked by a particular situation, a trigger argument or set of circumstances that give rise to frustration, anger and, ultimately, violence being used. For Madden-Dempsey, domestic violence in its weak sense refers to violence that is not undertaken to assert or sustain patriarchal power dynamics (2009, p. 126); meaning for the purpose of the male asserting his dominant status. These isolated instances of 'situational couple violence' may or may not repeat, and aside from the assault itself, couples are said to enjoy relatively harmonious relationships where violence is not used to 'reign terror' or as a 'relationship-wide attempt to control' (Johnson. 2010, pp. 11–12). Otherwise put, the 'violent incident' models appear to describe 'assault minus coercive control' (Wiener, 2017, p. 501). When certain domestic abuse is understood in this way, the traditional incident focus of the criminal law might not seem so ill-suited.

Yet Johnson and Madden-Dempsey's analysis – that situational couple violence describes a distinct phenomenon from coercive control – is not beyond criticism. When 'situational couple violence' repeats and especially when it

84   *Antonia Porter*

escalates into a chronic problem with increased brutality, to suggest that such abuse is merely episodic and a number of discrete occurrences seems disingenuous and belies how aspects of power and control may play out in between events. Walker's three phases of 'repetitious' or 'cyclical violence' – the tension-building phase; the violent incident; and the honeymoon phase – at least acknowledge that during the tension-building (but violence-free) phase, physiological strain and negative emotional and mental health harms can be experienced by the victim in anticipation of the violence (Walker, 2017, p. 97). Some women have even reported taking action to provoke the awaited violence due to the unbearable anticipation of it (Walker, 2017, p. 97).

However, Walker's cyclical model has also been criticised (Goodmark, 2009, p. 44; Wilson, 2019). The limitations of both Johnson's (repeated) 'situational couple violence' model and Walker's 'cycle of violence' are highlighted when considered against Stark's exposé of coercive control as a multidimensional oppression of personal life (2007, p. 10) and Pence et al.'s uncovering of an array of abusive tactics designed to control and assert power (1993, p. 2).

That coercive control is widely acknowledged as an ongoing or omnipresent 'strategy of domination' (Stark, 2012, p. 210; Stark, 2007) signals the theoretical evolution in understanding domestic abuse (Goodmark, 2009, p. 44). More recently, Walker's revised and updated model acknowledges the range of non-violent yet controlling behaviours perpetrators can inflict even in the 'reconciliation' phase of the cycle; 'sometimes what seemed so loving in one context actually seemed a continuation of the controlling and over possessive behaviour of the batterer' (Walker, 2017, p. 107). Similarly, one survivor explained to Pence that the violence in her relationship was not cyclical, because 'even when he is being nice to you, it's a part of the violence' (Pence, 2010).

'Emotional abuse' is at its most unambiguous when it is characterised by humiliating or degrading 'put-downs' and gendered criticisms which are objectively cruel. But the revelation that prosecutors might have to convey to a court that ostensibly kind gestures – moments of flattery, of attentiveness and even of loyalty – might also be characterised as *part* of the controlling or coercive behaviour is more nuanced and challenging. If prosecutors fail to expose that these behaviours can also be a component of the perpetrator's power and control, the alternative is that the defence team will point to these prima facie considerate and devoted actions to indicate that the relationship was healthy and without coercion or control.

The trial prosecutor will accordingly need to navigate and guide the triers of fact through the 'blurred boundaries' that exist between caring behaviours embodied within 'normal relationships' and the attentive, romantic and possessive behaviours manifest in coercive and controlling ones (Barlow and Walklate, 2022, p. 11). Once a relationship is established, a perpetrator might punctuate the abusive relationship with momentary flashbacks to the intense, seemingly romantic, courtship – or grooming – so many survivors describe at the outset of the relationship (Wiener, 2017, p. 507). In this context, gestures of 'kindness' might be better understood as a tool that keeps the victim-survivor close and which facilitates her obedience, the perpetrator's micromanagement of her behaviour and the deployment of '"rules" for everyday living' (Stark, 2012, p. 210). Her fear is often a key indicator of when this slippage has taken place (Barlow and Walklate, 2022, p. 11; Herring, 2020, p. 27). Through careful questioning, prosecutors will need to draw out why a victim-survivor believes that certain ostensibly considerate behaviours feel sinister or controlling and why once non-problematic conduct has become part of the problem (Barlow and Walklate, 2022, p. 11; Herring, 2020, p. 27).

With an awareness of this continuum of abuse in mind, the chapter now considers how the CPS prosecutor can evidence the requisite level of harm to the victim-survivor as set out in section 76 Serious Crime Act and how, in Northern Ireland, the PPS prosecutor can satisfy 'the reasonable person' to consider the course of behaviour likely to cause the victim-survivor physical or psychological harm, per section 1(2) of the legislation.

Pre-Charge Considerations: Selecting Charges and Dates

Whilst, as suggested earlier, there is scope to argue that repeated situational couple violence, absent other more overt coercive control strategies, may give rise to emotional tension and anticipatory anxiety for the victim, these responses may not meet the threshold for proving a criminal offence has occurred. To provide a 'realistic prospect of conviction' (CPS, 2018A; CPS, 2018B), a CPS prosecutor must be satisfied at the pre-charge stage that the prescribed level of harm is met (England and Wales). Specifically, section 76 Serious Crime Act 2015 requires that the behaviour had a 'serious effect' on the victim (namely that it caused her to fear, on at least two occasions, that violence would be used against her, or that it caused her serious alarm or distress which had a substantial adverse effect on her usual day-to-day activities). Conversely, to provide a 'reasonable prospect of conviction' (Public Prosecution Service, 2016), section 3(1) of the Domestic Abuse and Civil Proceedings Act (Northern Ireland) 2021 establishes that the offence can be committed whether or not the behaviour in question actually caused the victim to suffer harm; section 1 requiring that the behaviour must be such that a reasonable person would consider the course of behaviour *likely* to cause physical or psychological harm. Yet whilst it may appear that the Northern Irish offence avoids some of the difficulties that have arisen in England and Wales as regards establishing the *existential* impact on the victim-survivor, prosecutors in Northern Ireland would still benefit from approaching the case by establishing that harm has, in fact, been caused (where possible). For, if PPS prosecutors can evidence the actual harm caused, it facilitates establishing that

86 *Antonia Porter*

a reasonable person would consider the course of behaviour likely to cause physical or psychological harm.

In England and Wales, if, at the pre-charge stage, the statement taker has not explored how and to what extent the perpetrator's behaviour has harmed the victim, then the prosecutor will need to require the police to obtain a further statement requesting the complainant to describe the impact of the abuse on her. The harm element that *must* be proved in section 76 coercive control cases is likely to mirror the contents of a 'victim personal statement' (VPS). This statement is routinely taken in all criminal cases where there is an identifiable victim and is usually referred to by the prosecutor as part of the sentencing hearing.[5] Police are familiar with taking VPS statements which describe the physical, emotional, financial or other impacts the offence has had on the victim. In section 76 coercive control cases, the complainant's written statement *needs* to include the same information so that the prosecutor can assess the harm element of the offence. Northern Irish prosecutors would be well advised to obtain the same information to assist the triers of fact in determining whether the perpetrator's behaviour was *likely* to cause harm.

Once a prosecutor has satisfied themselves that behaviour on the requisite number of occasions[6] caused harm (or, in Northern Ireland, was likely to do so), a prosecutor should consider whether there are any particular events – such as a serious assault with use of a weapon – that merit a separate charge in addition to relying on it as part of the ongoing coercive control offence. A conviction for a stand-alone offence relating to a specific serious incident will have the effect of 'marking the card' of the offender's record of previous convictions. This may prove advantageous for both the sentencing exercise and also in the event that future partners should seek details of the offender's previous convictions under the Domestic Violence Disclosure Scheme 2014 in England and Wales or the Domestic Violence and Abuse Disclosure Scheme 2016 in Northern Ireland. If prosecutors prefer a separate date-specific charge, they will need to be satisfied that there is a realistic prospect of conviction in respect of coercive control with *or without* it (Jones v DPP [2011] 1 WLR 833).

A prosecutor will also need to select charge dates. No behaviours that took place prior to 29 December 2015 in England and Wales or 21 February 2022 in Northern Ireland may be included. Aside from that caveat, charges should 'facilitate the clear presentation of the case at court and accurately reflect the extent of the accused's involvement and responsibility, allowing the court appropriate sentencing powers' (CPS, 2017, p. 6). Over the course of a relationship that may have spanned years, facilitating a straightforward presentation of the case for the purpose of the trial at the same time as reflecting the extent of abuse experienced by the victim so that sentence can properly reflect the seriousness of the offence, may seem antithetical.

The strained ambitions of capturing the full (or sufficient) criminality of the behaviour on the one hand whilst ensuring a straightforward and comprehensible delivery of the case on the other are compounded by the added dimension of the managerial pressures brought to bear on prosecutors specifically (Hodgson, 2020, p. 142) and the justice system more generally (Hodgson, 2020, p. 13). Criminal courts are imbued with the lexicon of efficiency, particularly in the summary, criminal courts with voluminous caseloads where demands for expediency have only increased since the 1980s (Welsh and Howard, 2019, p. 796). Summary justice must be speedy and hearings 'simple' and 'accessible' (Auld, 2001, p. 271). With assorted directives asserting the efficiency priority, prosecutors will not be able to escape the expectation that cases should be expeditiously processed (Criminal Procedure Rules, 2020, 1.1(2)e; Ministry of Justice, 2013; Leveson, 2015). However, despite the context of expediency, prosecutors must be discouraged from cutting corners by restricting the charge period. Justice should not be compromised by prosecutors limiting the particulars of the offence or the scope of the facts merely to avoid lengthy contested hearings and the inevitable additional preparation work that comes with that.

Choosing which charge dates to prefer and which behaviours to include in the charge will naturally depend on the particular case. Overall, the charge dates should include sufficient scope to reflect the extent, duration, methods deployed and impact of the abuse and this ultimately will be a matter of judgement for the charging prosecutor. Whilst the sentencing guidelines issued by the Sentencing Council (Sentencing Council, 2018) are not applicable in Northern Ireland, the principles contained in them might act as a prompt when selecting charge dates and could be advantageous to the PPS. For example, for the offence, and consequently the sentence to reflect the highest culpability, prosecutors will need to select dates that capture that the behaviours were persistent, prolonged and deployed the use of multiple methods designed to humiliate and degrade the victim (Sentencing Council, 2018). To demonstrate the highest level of harm for sentencing purposes, the behaviour within the charge dates must have caused the victim to fear violence on 'many occasions' and caused her 'very serious alarm or distress which has a substantial adverse effect on the victim' (Sentencing Council, 2018).

Pre-Charge Disclosure

Despite the CPS only being responsible for the charging decision in 28% of cases, the police must always obtain prosecution pre-charge advice in coercive control cases in England and Wales (CPS, 2020). There is no parallel requirement in Northern Ireland. When consulted by police officers, the decision to charge or to request further investigation in anticipation of charge will be made by the prosecutor on the basis of written statements and other documentary or real evidence provided by the police. How to ensure the competence of the police statement taker to capture the extent and nuance of coercive control is beyond the scope of this chapter, but, clearly, adequate training

88 *Antonia Porter*

in respect of coercive control for those undertaking this aspect of the investigation is key for successful prosecutions. Particularly, where a not guilty plea is anticipated, even where the evidential threshold is met at the pretrial stage, prosecutors need to ensure that the police have pursued all reasonable lines of enquiry that point both towards or away from the suspect (Ministry of Justice, 2020, pp. 10–12; A-G Guidelines on Disclosure, 2022; Public Prosecution Service Code for Prosecutors, 2016, p. 24).[7] Such an approach would signal an occupational and cultural shift away from adversarial approaches to disclosure that some have argued have traditionally plagued investigators (Johnston, 2020, p. 18).

In anticipated contested cases, all material – including unused material – that will assist the defence with the early preparation of their defence or for the purposes of applying for bail ought to be available at the first court hearing in any event (MoJ, CPIA Codes of Practice, 2020, p. 10). Yet particularly in coercive control cases, prosecutors should anticipate that there will be relevant material contained on digital devices – for example, mobile phones or laptops – that may reveal, for example, the perpetrator's technological surveillance of the victim-survivor or the tenor of communication between parties (Havard and Lefevre, 2020). Digital material may either form part of the prosecution evidence or, conversely, it may serve to undermine it or assist the defence case (triggering its disclosure under section 3 CPIA 1996). Either way, the likely presence of digital material in a contested coercive control trial needs to be considered from the outset, pre-charge.

The prosecutor's disclosure obligations, however, do not give a carte blanche to the police to seize and interrogate a complainant's personal devices. Guidance from the Court of Appeal in R v Bater-James and R v Mohammed (Sultan) [2021] 1 WLR 725 makes clear that this will only be necessary in pursuit of a *reasonable* line of inquiry. Regard will be needed for the *prospect* of obtaining relevant material and the perceived *relevance* of that material in the context of the individual case (A-G Guidelines on Disclosure, 2022, p. 5). Should review of a witness's digital communications be necessary in light of the prosecution case or the defence forwarded in the police interview, then investigators should use the least intrusive means possible and adopt what the Court of Appeal has called an 'incremental approach' to obtaining the material (R v Bater-James). This means that investigators should be sure that recourse to the witness's device is the only option; that the device should be interrogated in limited part where possible; that the witness is minimally inconvenienced; and that appropriate redactions are made to the downloaded material (R v Bater-James).

This approach to unused digital material is intended to minimise the incursion into witness privacy, as balanced against the defendant's right to a fair trial (A-G Guidelines on disclosure, 2022, pp. 5–7). The balance to be struck is a delicate one as failure to adequately interrogate digital devices may prompt the defence to argue that the defendant can no longer enjoy a fair trial and that proceedings should be stayed as an abuse of process (R (Ebrahim) v Feltham Magistrates' Court [2001] 1 All ER 831). This is why obtaining unused material in a timely fashion is vital (though the court noted in Bater-James that a fair trial may still be possible if the trial process can compensate for the absence of such material through careful cross-examination of the complainant and judicial directions).

The Trial: Examining the Survivor in Chief

The coercive control offences criminalise the 'underlying architecture' of an abusive intimate relationship (Tolmie, 2018, p. 52). Prosecuting advocates are tasked with teasing out from the complainant how the perpetrator's behaviours constricted her freedoms, limited her options and made her feel trapped (Stark, 2007). The types of behaviours that underpin the abusive relationship will be 'culturally and contextually prescribed' (Velonis, 2016, p. 1036) and, accordingly, the prosecutor's role at trial will be to facilitate the factfinders 'to reorient themselves to the reality of victims' (Walklate et al., 2018, p. 122). Coercive control will be proved via a narrative account of the relationship and it is to the ways in which prosecutors might help survivors to convey their lived experience at trial that this chapter now turns.

In contested criminal proceedings, the complainant must provide a detailed account of her experience at two key moments: first to the police employee who writes her statement and second to the court when giving oral evidence at trial. The trial prosecutor relies on the content of the written statement to know the facts and details of the offence and to formulate the case narrative in advance. When the witness gives evidence in chief, ordinarily, and particularly if a statement is scant, the trial prosecutor will be reluctant to ask questions that might encourage recitation of information not contained in the statement. A primary rule of adversarial advocacy is to never ask a question to which you do not already know the answer (Morley, 2015, p. 238; McPeake, 2014, p. 150) lest the answer undermines your case or results in irrelevant digression. Perhaps most importantly, when a witness travels 'off script', the defence will likely put it to her in cross-examination and assert during the defence closing speech that the latest account aired in court has been fabricated at the moment and/or is evidence of witness unreliability.

Yet, over the course of an abusive relationship, illustrations of how the relationship was coercive or controlling are likely to be numerous and myriad. One remedy to avoid the witness revealing unanticipated facts in the witness box is to ensure police statement takers avoid taking incomplete statements; being fully trained and conversant with the tactics of perpetrators means that they will ask the victim appropriate yet discerning questions to extract the information. However, in practice where police statements remain sparse or inadequate, it is entirely possible that survivors will evidence further events, examples and explanations not included in their written account during the

90 *Antonia Porter*

course of their testimony. This will happen despite the complainant being given the opportunity to read and consult their written statement prior to trial and being asked questions designed to elicit the statement's contents (CPS, 2018C, 3.4C).

For this reason, prosecutors in coercive control cases might be advised to anticipate the surfacing of new revelations 'in chief'. These revelations are likely not only because of the frequency, duration and totality of the abuse the victim-survivor has experienced over the course of the relationship but also bearing in mind the effect that trauma and depression can have on memory recall. Depression, situational disorder and psychosis are common effects of being a victim of coercive control (Stark, 2007, p. 122; Kemp et al., 1991, p. 137). When a witness suffers mental ill-health and trauma, memories can be fragmented and dominated by sensorial, perceptual and emotional detail (Crespo and Fernández-Lansac, 2016). When a prosecutor probes into those details at trial, it is possible that the survivor will be triggered or prompted to recall additional behaviours not previously disclosed.

Whilst, typically, the prosecutor will want to avert novel revelations from a witness 'in chief' due to concerns they will have about the inevitable defence assertions that the witness is unreliable, exaggerating or biased, in coercive control cases prosecutors might instead choose to anticipate novel revelations and to work with the complainant to furnish the court with further details. Though it runs counter to common practice, coercive control trials may merit the prosecutor 'loosening the reins' when the complainant is giving evidence. Prosecutors can address in their closing speech any attacks the defence makes on the victim-survivor's credibility by suggesting that such revelations are to be entirely expected in these cases for the reasons outlined earlier. The approach may also carry advantages for the complainant as the court will hear evidence that is unrehearsed and may be persuasive and compelling as a result.

Prosecutors in England and Wales and also in Northern Ireland should be mindful that when evidencing coercive control, 'context is everything' (Stark, 2007, p. 309) and in the criminal courts more often than not the complainant will carry the burden of narrating that context. Prosecutors will need to help the witness paint a picture of the relationship and the atmosphere in which she was living. Context will explain why certain objectively and ostensibly innocuous perpetrator actions were, for that complainant, coercive or controlling. By illustration, Wiener's work recounts how one perpetrator strangled his wife with a bathroom towel, after which he never used violence in the relationship again. For that couple, simple production of a towel at 'pinch points' in the relationship became laden with symbolism and menace (Wiener, 2017, p. 507). For a lay bystander, absent the context, the gesture would have appeared harmless and, without context, the risk for a woman recounting an incident in which the perpetrator placed a towel on a table is that she presents as irrational and overstating his coercion of her. With context, her logical and explicable fear can be conveyed to the court.

'Successful' Coercive Control Prosecutions   91

To ensure that full context is exposed and explained to the court, a simple strategy a trial prosecutor might adopt is to simply ask the complainant not only to describe what happened and how it made her feel but also *why* it made her feel scared, anxious, angry or trapped. This additional question may prompt an explanation that has hitherto been hidden or merely implied; it may prompt the complainant to explain (possibly for the first time) why his leaving a towel on the table was significant and probative of the offence. Allowing the complainant to articulate why the behaviour made her feel a certain way helps to 'sure up' the requirement of proving that the offence had a 'serious effect' (section 76 Serious Crime Act 2015) or would cause a reasonable person to conclude the behaviour likely to cause physical or psychological harm (section 1(2) Domestic Abuse and Criminal Proceedings Act (Northern Ireland) 2021).

Problems may also arise for the trial prosecutor should the complainant, whilst giving evidence, refer to the defendant's 'bad character' that occurred outside of the chosen charge dates. 'Bad character' refers to any 'evidence of or disposition towards misconduct [the commission of an offence or other reprehensible behaviour] other than which has to do with the alleged facts or the offence with which the defendant is charged' (section 98 Criminal Justice Act 2003; Article 3 Criminal Justice (Evidence) (Northern Ireland) Order 2004). Ordinarily, defence objections to assertions that amount to 'bad character' would rightly result in a prosecutor advising the witness to answer the question that has specifically been put (so as to avoid the witness attacking the defendant's character). However, if the revelations further example the defendant's coercive control and are consequently probative and relevant, and the risk of the complainant's own character being introduced is considered in the balance, there is scope for a prosecutor to do two things. Either, the prosecutor could argue that the revelations fall outside of the 'bad character' regime as they have 'to do with the alleged facts', that is, the defendant's coercive control of the complainant and should therefore be permitted (and it is suggested here that this argument is likely to be stronger in coercive control cases given the 'ongoing' nature of the relationship). Or, alternatively, the prosecutor could apply for the bad character to be adduced (section 101(1) (d) Criminal Justice Act 2003 or Article 6(1)(d) Criminal Justice (Evidence) (Northern Ireland) Order 2004) to show that the defendant has a propensity to behave in the way alleged in the charge. The fact that the previous behaviour has not resulted in a conviction is not a bar to it being adduced; mere allegations of criminal offences can be adduced (R v Z [2000] 2 AC 483; R v Terry [2005] QB 996) or other reprehensible behaviour that falls short of a criminal offence (R v M [2014] Crim 823; R v Donnelley [2006] EWCA Crim 545).

In proceeding on a basis that enables the complainant's 'expansive' oral testimony, the prosecuting advocate might be reminded of two overriding concepts. First, as the complainant is the principal prosecution witness and the prosecuting authority has made the decision to pursue the case, prosecutors

92 Antonia Porter

ought to feel comfortable treating her as a 'witness of truth' rather than as someone whose account needs to be constrained and limited. Second, the prosecutor's role is as an independent officer of the court. Their job is to assist the triers of fact to convict the guilty and to acquit the innocent; their role differs from the partisan defence barrister who is instructed to advance zealously their client's case. The prosecutor in that context merely offers the opportunity for the complainant to assist the court.

The Trial: The Prosecutor as Expert

Relevant expert evidence may be relied upon by a party to proceedings on any matter calling for expertise that is *necessarily* outside of the everyday knowledge and understanding of the triers of fact (R v Turner [1975] 1 All ER 70). Whether a subject area falls within the common experience and awareness of the triers of fact is not something that will always carry a clear answer. It may be that an 'educative judicial direction' could render expert evidence nugatory (Keane and McKeown, 2022, p. 652) or that a successful argument could be made that juries are able to evaluate for themselves whether, for example, a relationship dynamic is healthy and, conversely then, which behaviours fall outside of those parameters and cause the victim harm. The guidance for Crown Prosecutors (CPS, 2017; Public Prosecution Service, 2022) remains silent about whether prosecutors should consider instructing an expert in coercive control cases.

The question of *who* demonstrates sufficient competence to act as an expert in the field of coercive control is ultimately for the trial judge to determine. Where experts are without formal professional qualifications, courts have typically been generous in their interpretation of who has the requisite skills and experience (R v Silverlock [1894] 2 QB 766; R v Dallagher [2003] 1 Cr App R 195). In practice, those regularly working with survivors and perpetrators would likely be eligible, as would policymakers and researchers working in the field. Overall, the criminal courts are known to have a liberal approach to the admissibility of expert evidence (Roberts, 2008) and have correspondingly shown themselves to be amenable to hearing from coercive control experts in cases where survivors have killed their abusive partners (even if the expert's impact in securing positive outcomes for the abused woman who kills has thus far been negligible) (Bettinson, 2019; Barlow and Walklate, 2022, p. 67).[8]

A coercive control expert could assist the court in determining when a relationship stops being 'normal' and 'abuse' begins (Tolmie, 2018, p. 56). Coercive control experts would have the role of explaining the social phenomena; of outlining the victim's experience; of explaining that victim responses are varied; and would be able to differentiate the victim's response to the abusive behaviour as distinct from any pre-existing pathological conditions (Henaghan, 2022). By drawing on a framework that takes into account the entire relationship history, coercive control experts would be able to 'widen the legal lens, bringing context into view' and explain what might otherwise have appeared irrational victim behaviour (Tuerkheimer, 2003, pp. 999–1000).

Expert evidence about the contours and forces at work within coercive relationships would likely assist the triers of fact in noticing the perpetrator's strategies and understanding how the abuse impacted the victim-survivor. Experts would be able to direct the court to consider not just specific events or moments of tension described by the complainant but could also invite the court to notice the interim dynamic. We know that coercive and controlling abuse can be difficult to recognise for both the survivor and the bystander as behaviours that amount to an offence may appear innocuous (Wiener, 2017, p. 509). The micro-regulations of daily activities (Stark, 2007) are made even more invisible within the context of 'traditional' gendered roles and perpetrators' exploitation of prevailing gender norms such as women's roles as mothers, homemakers and wives. If the perpetrator's micromanagement of the victim may have been imperceptible to the victim and third-party witnesses, it may also appear 'inoffensive' to the triers of fact who will likely be scrutinising the evidence through the lens of society's prevalent unequal power relations. An expert witness may help to re-frame the narrative, call out misogyny, explain why a woman reacted to certain behaviours in the way she did and explain to a lay jury why she felt unable to leave (Hanna, 2009, p. 1470).

Yet, trial prosecutors will always be left with the pragmatic reality that such experts are rarely if ever instructed, funded or available. Absent an expert, trial lawyers might instead choose to act as experts by proxy; in opening, in examination of witnesses and in closing. Throughout the trial, prosecutors might seek out opportunities to present the case and the defendant's behaviours through the lens of Stark's work. In opening, the prosecutor has the opportunity to explain the case theory and to focus minds on how the evidence will prove the perpetrator's coercion of the victim. Through a non-contentious summary of the facts, prosecutors can frame the case 'issue' and tackle head-on anticipated and unfavourable narratives the defence will rely on. For example, 'attentive' text messages can be suggested as tools of control, opportunities permitted to the victim to socialise with family become the perpetrator's means of keeping her family in the dark and the perpetrator permitting the victim to work a means of his controlling her whereabouts. When examining the defendant, prosecutors might seek to expose his misogyny, his gendered role expectations and his various techniques of and motives for control. Finally, in closing, through inference, suggestion and proposition, prosecutors can show how the perpetrator drew the victim in close and how he used confounding means to keep it that way.

Conclusion

An expansive inquiry into the modus operandi of the perpetrator is more likely to capture the extent and duration of his coercive control than a

94   *Antonia Porter*

reductive exercise into two or more specific incidents. Prosecutors, however, find themselves working within a justice process that demands expedience and a subsequent fact-finding procedure – the criminal trial – that is typically de-contextualised in focus. Pushing against the resulting cultural inclination to confine the facts-in-issue to specific (albeit maybe repeated) violent incidents is required. Any predisposition to condense the woman's experience out of professional habit is further compounded by managerial demands. Prosecutors will be conditioned to adopt practices that facilitate proficient case preparation and presentation (Porter, 2020), within a system that must process voluminous caseloads within tightly constrained budgets (Auld, 2001; MoJ, 2013; Leveson, 2015; Hodgson, 2020). As such, expansive examination of the abusive relationship that contextualises the victim's experience will contrast, even conflict, with the cultural grain.

To assist in achieving the convictions that both the CPS and PPS are committed to, the chapter has urged prosecutors to become experts in the forms of oppression and domination that characterise coercive control. Conversance with the impact on victims is also required so that cases can be presented with an unambiguous narrative capable of proving the harm, or likely harm, elements of the offence (McGorrery and McMahon, 2019, p. 957). The chapter has outlined that the need for a coherent case strategy begins pre-charge; ensuring timely disclosure of material, especially digital material, that may or may not remain unused. Moreover, charge dates ought to reflect the extent of the problem and offer sufficient scope for sentencers. The chapter has also suggested ways that the trial prosecutor – during speeches and examination of witnesses – can shift attention from the specific incident(s) to facilitating the victim to narrate the context and her reality.

This chapter has explored some of the ways that prosecutors might, whilst working within the confines of the criminal justice system, assist women survivors to access justice. Yet the chapter concludes by reiterating its opening caveat that 'justice' might not mean achieving a conviction wherever possible, despite institutional performance monitoring that might signal to prosecutors otherwise. Whilst the new coercive control laws might be considered progressive in, inter alia, their potential to offer recognition and affirmation for many controlled women, the laws only represent an advance for women to the extent that they are responsive to their needs (Schneider, 2008). If cases proceed absent a woman's support, there is a danger that the law overrides and defines women's subjectivities in ways that do not serve them individually or collectively (Smart, 2002, p. 25; Porter, 2020, p. 19). Whilst prosecutors should ensure that they expertly prepare and present the case in the manner contemplated here, they must only proceed absent the survivor's support where her safety, material and emotional needs are not compromised. Moreover, even where survivors are committed to prosecution, if, by having criminalised coercive control, the state in any way reneges on addressing gender-based abuse

'Successful' Coercive Control Prosecutions   95

through means other than the criminal law, then any advances in the criminal law will not have been worth the price paid.

Notes

1 S. 76 Serious Crime Act 2015, as amended by s. 68 Domestic Abuse Act 2021. A and B are now 'personally connected' if they are, *or have been*, married/in a civil partnership or agreement/engaged/in an intimate relationship/relatives or have had parental relationship with regard to the same child.
2 As found in s. 1 Domestic Abuse and Civil Proceedings Act (Northern Ireland) 2021.
3 Between 97% and 99% of perpetrators were male in 2016–2019 (MoJ, 2019).
4 Admission of previous bad character is subject to admission under s. 98–103 Criminal Justice Act 2003; art 3 Criminal Justice (Evidence) (Northern Ireland) Order 2004.
5 Victim Personal Statements were first announced in the Victim's Charter 1996 and were introduced in England and Wales in October 2001 in 'Practice Direction-Crime Victim Personal Statements' (2001) 4 All ER 640: III 28. In Northern Ireland, victim personal statements were put on a statutory footing in sections 33–35 of the Justice Act (Northern Ireland) 2015, and are included in section 3 of the NI Victim Charter, available at <www.justice-ni.gov.uk/sites/default/files/publications/doj/victim-charter.pdf> accessed 9 September 2022.
6 In England and Wales, s. 76 details the behaviour must be 'repeated or continuous' and in Northern Ireland s 1 requires there must be 'two or more occasions' of coercive or controlling behaviour.
7 Exceptionally, when a decision is made for reasons of expediency where the suspect's remand into custody is sought, prosecutors may make the decision to charge on the 'threshold test', in which case further lines of enquiry may still need to be pursued at the behest of the prosecutor and kept under continuous review (A-G Guidelines on Disclosure, 2022, p. 17).
8 Notably, Professor Evan Stark was permitted to give evidence in Sally Challen's appeal to explain the part that the deceased's control over the appellant throughout their relationship might have played in his killing.

References

Attorney General (2022) *Guidelines on Disclosure*. London: Attorney General's Office.
Auld, R. (2001) *Review of the Criminal Courts of England and Wales: Report*. London: Stationery Office Books (TSO).
Barlow, C. (2019) 'Policing Coercive Control Project Report', https://eprints.lancs.ac.uk/id/eprint/135955/1/Policing_Coercive_Control_Project_Report_final.pdf.
Barlow, C. and Walklate, S. (2022) *Coercive Control*. Abingdon: Routledge.
Bettinson, V. (2019) 'Aligning the Partial Defence to Murder with Coercive Controlling Behaviour', *Journal of Criminal Law*, 83, pp. 71–86.
Crespo, M. and Fernández-Lansac, V. (2016) 'Memory and Narrative of Traumatic Events: A Literature Review', *Psychological Trauma: Theory, Research, Practice, and Policy*, 8, pp. 149–156.
Crossman, K.A. and Hardesty, J.L. (2018) 'Placing Coercive Control at the Center: What Are the Processes of Coercive Control and What Makes Control Coercive?', *Psychology of Violence*, 8, pp. 196–206.

96 *Antonia Porter*

Crown Prosecution Service (2016) *Violence against Women and Girls Strategy: 2017–20*, www.cps.gov.uk/publication/violence-against-women-and-girls.

Crown Prosecution Service (2017) *Legal Guidance: Controlling or Coercive Behaviour in an Intimate or Family Relationship*, www.cps.gov.uk/legal-guidance/controlling-or-coercive-behaviour-intimate-or-family-relationship.

Crown Prosecution Service (2018A) *About Charging*, www.cps.gov.uk/about/charging.html.

Crown Prosecution Service (2018B) *The Code for Prosecutors*, www.cps.gov.uk/publication/code-crown-prosecutors.

Crown Prosecution Service (2018C) *Legal Guidance: Speaking to Witnesses at Court*, www.cps.gov.uk/legal-guidance/speaking-witnesses-court.

Crown Prosecution Service (2020) *Charging (The Director's Guidance)*, www.cps.gov.uk/legal-guidance/charging-directors-guidance-sixth-edition-december-2020#Annex1.

Dempsey, M.M. (2009) *Prosecuting Domestic Violence: A Philosophical Analysis*. Oxford: Oxford University Press.

Douglas, H. (2008) 'The Criminal Law's Response to Domestic Violence: What's Going on?', *Sydney Law Review*, 30, pp. 439–469.

Goodmark, L. (2009) 'Reframing Domestic Violence Law and Policy: An Anti-Essentialist Proposal', *Washington University Journal of Law and Policy*, 31, pp. 39–56.

Hanna, C. (2009) 'The Paradox of Progress: Translating Evan Stark's Coercive Control into Legal Doctrine for Abused Women', *Violence against Women*, 15, pp. 1458–1476.

Havard, T.E. and Lefevre, M. (2020) 'Beyond the Power and Control Wheel: How Abusive Men Manipulate Mobile Phone Technologies to Facilitate Coercive Control', *Journal of Gender Based Violence*, 4, pp. 223–239.

Henaghan, M., Short, J. and Gulliver, P. (2022) 'Family Violence Experts in the Criminal Court: The Need to Fill the Void', *Psychiatry, Psychology and Law*, 29, pp. 206–222.

Herring, J. (2020) *Domestic Abuse and Human Rights*. Cambridge: Intersentia.

Hodgson, J.S. (2020) *The Metamorphosis of Criminal Justice: A Comparative Account*. Oxford: Oxford University Press.

Home Office (2015) *Controlling or Coercive Behaviour Now a Crime*, www.gov.uk/government/news/coercive-or-controlling-behaviour-now-a-crime.

Home Office (2021) *Guidance: Review of the Coercive or Controlling Behaviour Offence*, www.gov.uk/government/publications/review-of-the-controlling-or-coercive-behaviour-offence/review-of-the-controlling-or-coercive-behaviour-offence.

Johnson, M.P. (2010) *A Typology of Domestic Violence: Intimate Terrorism, Violent Resistance, and Situational Couple Violence*. Boston: Northeastern University Press.

Johnston, E. (2020) 'The Rise of Managerialism: The Impact of Swift and (Un) Sure Justice on Disclosure in Criminal Proceedings', in Johnston, E. and Smith, T. (eds.) *The Law of Disclosure*. Abingdon: Routledge, pp. 3–18.

Keane, A. and McKeown, P. (2022) *The Modern Law of Evidence* (14th ed.). Oxford: Oxford University Press.

Kemp, A., Rawlings, E.I. and Green, B.L. (1991) 'Post-Traumatic Stress Disorder (PTSD) in Battered Women: A Shelter Sample', *Journal of Traumatic Stress*, 4, pp. 137–148.

Leveson, B. (2015) *Review of Efficiency in Criminal Proceedings*. Judiciary of England and Wales, https://www.judiciary.uk/wp-content/uploads/2015/01/review-of-efficiency-in-criminal-proceedings-20151.pdf.

McGorrery, P. and McMahon, M. (2019) 'Criminalising" the Worst" Part: Operationalising the Offence of Coercive Control in England and Wales', *Criminal Law Review*, 11, pp. 957–965.

McPeake, R. (2014) *Advocacy*. Oxford: Oxford University Press.

Ministry of Justice (2013) *Transforming the CJS: A Strategy and Action Plan to Reform the Criminal Justice System*. London: HMSO.

Ministry of Justice (2020) *Criminal Procedure and Investigations Act 1996 (Section 23(1)) Code of Practice Revised in Accordance with Section 25(4) of the Criminal Procedure and Investigations Act 1996*. London: HMSO.

Morley, I. (2015) *The Devil's Advocate*. London: Sweet and Maxwell.

Office for National Statistics (2021) *Domestic Abuse Prevalence and Trends, England and Wales: Year Ending March 2021*, www.ons.gov.uk/peoplepopulationandcommunity/crimeandjustice/articles/domesticabuseprevalenceandtrendsenglandandwales/yearendingmarch2021.

Pence, E. (2010) 'Ellen Pence, Battered Women's Leader', *Video*, www.youtube.com/watch?v=r9dZOgr78eE.

Pence, E., Paymar, M. and Ritmeester, T. (1993) *Education Groups for Men Who Batter: The Duluth Model*. New York: Springer Publishing Company.

Porter, A. (2020) *Prosecuting Domestic Abuse in Neoliberal Times*. London: Palgrave Macmillan.

Public Prosecution Service (2016) *Code for Prosecutors*, https://www.ppsni.gov.uk/files/ppsni/publications/PPS%20Code%20for%20Prosecutors.pdf.

Public Prosecution Service (2022) *Domestic Violence and Abuse*, www.ppsni.gov.uk/domestic-violence-and-abuse.

Roberts, A. (2008) 'Drawing on Expertise: Legal Decision-Making and the Reception of Expert Evidence', *Criminal Law Review*, 6, pp. 443–462.

Rollinson, M. (2000) 'Re-Reading Criminal Law: Gendering the Mental Element', in Nicolson, D. and Bibbings, L. (eds.) *Feminist Perspectives on Criminal Law*. London: Routledge-Cavendish, p. 101.

Schneider, E.M. (2008) *Battered Women and Feminist Lawmaking*. New Haven: Yale University Press.

Sentencing Council (2018) *Controlling or Coercive Behaviour in an Intimate or Family Relationship*, www.sentencingcouncil.org.uk/offences/magistrates-court/item/controlling-or-coercive-behaviour-in-an-intimate-or-family-relationship/.

Smart, C. (2002) *Feminism and the Power of Law*. Abingdon: Routledge.

Stark, E. (2007) *Coercive Control: How Men Entrap Women in Personal Life*. Oxford: Oxford University Press.

Stark, E. (2012) 'Looking beyond Domestic Violence: Policing Coercive Control', *Journal of Police Crisis Negotiations*, 12, pp. 199–217.

Tolmie, J.R. (2018) 'Coercive Control: To Criminalize or Not to Criminalize?', *Criminology and Criminal Justice*, 18, pp. 50–66.

Tuerkheimer, D. (2003) 'Recognizing and Remedying the Harm to Battering: A Call to Criminalize Domestic Violence', *Journal of Criminal Law and Criminology*, 94, pp. 959–1032.

Velonis, A.J. (2016) '"He Never Did Anything You Typically Think of as Abuse" Experiences with Violence in Controlling and Non-Controlling Relationships in a Non-Agency Sample of Women', *Violence Against Women*, 22, pp. 1031–1054.

98 *Antonia Porter*

Walker, L.E.A. (2017) *The Battered Women Syndrome* (4th ed.). New York: Springer Publishing Company.

Walklate, S., Fitz-Gibbon, K. and McCulloch, J. (2018) 'Is More Law the Answer? Seeking Justice for Victims of Intimate Partner Violence through the Reform of Legal Categories', *Criminology and Criminal Justice*, 18, pp. 115–131.

Welsh, L. and Howard, M. (2019) 'Standardization and the Production of Justice in Summary Criminal Courts: A Post-Human Analysis', *Social and Legal Studies*, 28, pp. 774–793.

Wiener, C. (2017) 'Seeing What Is "Invisible in Plain Sight": Policing Coercive Control', *The Howard Journal of Crime and Justice*, 56, pp. 500–515.

Wiener, C. (2020) 'From Social Construct to Legal Innovation: The Offence of Controlling or Coercive Behaviour in England and Wales', in McMahon, M. and McGorrery, P. (eds.) *Criminalising Coercive Control: Family Violence and the Criminal Law*. Singapore: Springer, pp. 159–175.

Wilson, J.K. (2019) 'Cycle of Violence', in Bernat, F.P. and Frailing, K. (eds.) *The Encyclopedia of Women and Crime*. New Jersey: Wiley-Blackwell, pp. 1–5.

7 Taking Learnings From Other Jurisdictions on Supporting Victims and Survivors of Coercive Control

Sonya McMullan

The systematic dismantling of a woman piece by piece'
Voice of a Survivor from the WAFNI, Hear Her Voice Project of 2021

Women's Aid Federation Northern Ireland (Women's Aid NI) is the lead agency in Northern Ireland (NI) tackling domestic violence and abuse. For over 40 years, it has provided emergency accommodation and outreach/community services to support women, children and young people. The organisation works directly with women who have experienced intimate partner violence and through their lived experiences it is apparent that many women often do not know which service is appropriate for their specific needs or indeed if what they are experiencing is domestic abuse. Women may have problems identifying and naming their abuse if it is not physical in nature, however, domestic abuse encapsulates a wide range of behaviours which contribute to long-term trauma impacting on the whole family unit.

If women do not define their experiences as domestic abuse, it is unlikely that they will go on to report the crime and seek support. To prevent the cycle of abuse from continuing, we need early intervention and better inter-agency risk assessment so as a sector we can support these women in accessing services dedicated to their needs. Coercive control is one of the most under-reported crimes; it is often invisible and not always recognised as a criminal offence by the victims and survivors themselves. The challenge for practitioners is therefore making this crime more visible.

According to Police Service of Northern Ireland (PSNI) statistics, there were 33,186 domestic abuse incidents recorded in Northern Ireland from July 2021 to June 2022 (PSNI, 2022). However, it is difficult to get an accurate figure as to the number of families affected by domestic abuse in NI. Women's Aid Federation NI's Annual Report for 2020–2021 (Women's Aid NI, 2021B) shows that the organisation supported 6,005 women and 6,450 children within their community-based support, and that 530 women and 319 children stayed in emergency accommodation from April 2020 to March 2021. Women's Aid

DOI: 10.4324/9781003345305-7

100 *Sonya McMullan*

continues to provide frontline support in the face of more political instability and an insecure funding climate.

What Is Coercive Control?

Women's Aid NI defines coercive control as

> an intentional pattern of behaviour (often used alongside other forms of abuse) which can include threats, excessive regulation, intimidation, humiliation and enforced isolation. It is designed to punish, dominate, exploit, exhaust, create fear, confusion and increase dependency in a woman (or a woman and her children). Over time it can lead to a complete loss of self.[1]

This controlling behaviour is designed to make a person dependent on their abuser by isolating them from family, friends and support services, exploiting them, humiliating and degrading them and regulating their everyday behaviour. It can be a gradual process which over time can lead to a total loss of confidence and sense of self. We know in Women's Aid that most women experiencing domestic abuse are victims of coercive control. With the new domestic abuse offence, it is hoped that we will learn to better recognise patterns of perpetrator behaviour. We also need to see the coercive control offence being used when there has been no physical violence; then we will know the law is really working to protect victims of a crime, the effects of which are just as devastating as those of physical abuse.

Challenges

There are many challenges to the success of the domestic abuse offence in NI – some of these challenges are faced by other jurisdictions from which learnings can be taken. The main challenge that will be addressed within this chapter is the need for a gendered approach to domestic abuse. We need to use a gendered analysis to better support victims and survivors and this needs to be acknowledged by policymakers in NI, which requires a huge shift.

The issue of identification and recognition of coercive control is paramount, not only by public services and support agencies but by individuals themselves who sometimes do not recognise coercive control as a form of domestic abuse. There is of course much work to do in relation to the response of agencies through training and development in order to ensure appropriate responses to all victims and survivors of coercive control. The issue of public attitudes towards coercive control and societal change is paramount within the challenges faced. Finally, the area of prosecution of this crime is challenging, given that evidence of coercive control may be difficult to gather in order to prove a case in a court of law.

The Need for a Gendered Policy Approach

In NI for the last 12 years, domestic abuse has been dealt with through the policy directive of gender neutrality. The policy document titled 'Tackling Violence at Home – A Strategy for Addressing Domestic Violence and Abuse in Northern Ireland', which was produced by the Department of Health and Social Services and the Northern Ireland Office in 2005, took a gender-neutral approach to the issue of domestic abuse. However, it is a fact that women are overwhelmingly the victims of family violence and men are overwhelmingly the perpetrators. Crime data from England and Wales allows us to examine the gendered nature of coercive control. In England and Wales for the year ending December 2018, the majority of defendants prosecuted for controlling or coercive behaviour were male (97%), and the average custodial sentence given was 20 months. During that year, 308 offenders were sentenced for coercive and controlling behaviour. Of these offenders, 305 were male, one was female and the gender of the remaining two offenders was unknown (ONS, 2019). One study of data from the Crime Survey for England and Wales found that women are far more likely than men to be victims of abuse that involves ongoing degradation and frightening threats – two key elements of coercive control (Myhill, 2015). Despite this data, there has been no gendered policy approach to the issue or measuring of risk through a gendered lens. Women's Aid NI has continued to challenge this at every level including through the launch of a public campaign for a Violence Against Women and Girls (VAWG) Strategy on 8 March 2021.[2] An online petition in support of such a strategy received over 25,000 signatures of support.

Adopting a gendered analysis helps shine a light on the causes and consequences of violence and abuse which are different for men than they are for women, as are the type of approaches and support that are likely to be effective in preventing and eliminating it. Women's Aid has a key role to play in helping to ensure that a gendered analysis of violence and abuse is understood and adopted in all forms of VAWG. This includes ensuring gender equality is promoted in local policy and practice and in supporting the work of colleagues in both the voluntary and statutory sectors. Therefore, Women's Aid campaigned for a VAWG strategy in NI, which is the only part of the UK and Ireland not to have a strategy in place, and work is ongoing with the Executive Office to implement such a strategy. Women's Aid also emphasises that a strategy tackling gender-based violence will not discount the valid experiences of other gender identities, but instead will address the reality of the situation which is that women and girls are disproportionately affected. Using a gendered analysis means that the issues do not just sit with the Department of Justice and Department of Health but instead, a coordinated, multi-sectoral, cross-departmental approach is required. This means considering how policy and practice in areas such as early years, education, employment, health, housing and welfare impact on women's lives. Decision-makers can focus

102 *Sonya McMullan*

on working within these areas to see what they can do to deal with the root cause and tackle gender inequality and power imbalance. VAWG is a cause and consequence of gender inequality. To effectively tackle it, there is a need to address the social, cultural, economic and political inequalities that women currently experience within society.

The dynamics and impact of domestic abuse on women and girls must be explicitly recognised by our local Assembly, either by inclusion in the Stopping Domestic and Sexual Violence and Abuse Strategy or within the proposed VAWG Strategy. The current Domestic and Sexual Abuse Strategy (Department of Health, Social Services and Public Safety and Department of Justice, 2016) was for seven years (2016–2023) and is now out for consultation again. The Strategy is constructed around five key strands which focus on leadership, prevention, support, services and justice. Within these strands, 20 priority areas were highlighted for implementation throughout the life of the Strategy. The Northern Ireland Executive has directed that a Strategy to End Violence Against Women and Girls be developed, and the Executive Office is leading this work across departments. A programme of engagement and research is underway to inform the co-design process, and the Strategy will identify actions to tackle all kinds of offences, ranging from micro-aggressions and misogyny, through to violent and abusive behaviour directed at women and girls precisely because they are women and girls. This includes crimes and unwanted behaviour in the physical and online world.[3]

Women's Aid is of the view that any definition of domestic abuse should acknowledge that these crimes disproportionately affect women and girls and should explicitly name the gendered nature of domestic abuse to truly reflect the reality of the crime. Domestic abuse is a form of violence against women – a cause and consequence of women's inequality. Not only are women far more likely to be victims and men perpetrators, but women overwhelmingly experience coercive control within a context of fear. Without recognition of gender, the disproportionate scale and impact of domestic abuse on women will not be consistently understood (Aldridge, 2021). In NI, the local government has a 'gender-neutral' approach to domestic abuse, which obscures the reality of how abuse is perpetrated, who the victims and perpetrators are most likely to be, and what gender-specific services are required to meet the needs of both male and female victims.

Recognising and Responding to Coercive Control

[T]he invisible bruises can be a bit more hard to explain. Or hard to, not convince people, but, you know [they think], 'Oh yeah, it was domestic abuse', but when I say domestic violence the first thing they want to know is 'What, did he beat you?' I said, 'No, not with his hands or fists. Pushed and shoved, but emotionally, I'd been beaten.' 'Ah well, it's not really violence then'.

Voice of a Survivor from the WAFNI, Hear Her Voice Project of 2021

Taking Learnings From Other Jurisdictions 103

Women often have problems identifying and naming their abuse. This can be because of how the public perceives coercive control within the context of domestic abuse. If women do not define their experiences as domestic abuse, it is unlikely that they will go on to report the crime and seek support. In order to prevent the cycle of abuse from continuing, there is a need for early intervention and better inter-agency risk assessment, so that women can be supported in accessing services dedicated to their needs.

Many women feel that the term 'domestic violence' does not encompass their lived experience of coercive control. Language is important and using the term 'violence' to describe their experience can fail to acknowledge all the other forms of non-physical abuse that women experience daily. The Women's Aid NI 'Hear Her Voice' project[4] aimed to capture the lived experiences of domestic abuse survivors in Northern Ireland. Ninety-one women participated in 'Hear Her Voice'. The participation of these profoundly courageous, creative and intelligent women belies the notion that there is any 'typical' survivor of domestic abuse. The women were mothers, grandmothers, nurses, teachers, retirees, care workers, lecturers and managers, among others. Each of their voices was unique, and their stories their own, but they combine into a chorus which tells of our institutional and societal failings towards domestic abuse survivors in particular, and women in general. Survivors participating in this project felt the term 'domestic abuse' more accurately captured their lived experience and that it encapsulated a wider range of behaviours than 'domestic violence'. Language is key and we do not want to create silence when discussing domestic abuse and non-physical forms of harm, which according to survivors are as detrimental and traumatic as physical harm – we can fail to acknowledge the invisible bruises. These invisible bruises can include emotional and verbal abuse, isolation, online and cyber abuse, stalking, intimate partner sexual abuse and financial abuse (Snyder, 2020). Through the use of language, we can close off potential opportunities for disclosure and for women to recognise the harm they are experiencing and the opportunities for intervention and support.

A survivor participating in the 'Hear Her Voice' project stated that:

> It starts with the emotional anyway. I think the main thing to do with abuse is emotional. I feel like that's where it all starts, and that's where it will end . . . And that's what you have to deal with for the rest of your life. Because no matter how long we are out of our journey, I feel like that's always going to be in your head . . . But for me, like that's a challenge every day, is your emotional side of things . . . The physical – that's what I felt like, if he had kicked me, or done something bad to me, I might have said, 'Right, that's it, I'm gone.' Or someone might see something that they could come to me, and then I would open up to them. I had none of that. So I didn't have the option of anyone seeing it that would make me question. So when it's all emotional you're dealing with it all on your own. And it's

104   *Sonya McMullan*

a battle the whole time, because they [the perpetrator] have you thinking that you're absolutely crazy. And then you're battling it yourself in your head and you can't tell anyone about it.

Through the work of Women's Aid, women's silence can be broken and their stories can be shared. The voice of the survivor is so important for everyone to hear, to listen to and to learn from. That is why survivor engagement is one of the key principles of Women's Aid NI's new strategic plan, which states that 'Women, children and young people are at the heart of everything we do, and we will ensure our work is informed by their voices and experience' (Women's Aid NI, 2021A, p. 2).

Under section 32(1) of the Domestic Abuse and Civil Proceedings Act (NI) 2021, the PSNI and the Public Prosecution Service (PPS) must provide training for their personnel on the new domestic abuse offence, as must 'any additional body that has functions within the criminal justice system in Northern Ireland and which the Department of Justice specifies in connection with this section in regulations'. The legislation does not therefore provide that such training is mandatory for the judiciary or any other agencies including within the health and social care and education sectors. However, training for such agencies is key as there are frequent opportunities to assess and identify coercive and controlling behaviours within these sectoral roles. There is an urgent need for all first responders to know what coercive and controlling behaviours are, what questions to ask to identify this crime and what the appropriate pathways are to respond to it. Training in isolation is not however adequate in itself. For example, Waalen et al. (2000) found that education alone is insufficient and that institutional policies may constitute important barriers that must be addressed to affect actual practice behaviour.

When someone is experiencing domestic abuse, it is vital for an accurate and fast assessment of the danger to be made, so that help can be given as quickly as possible. One of the tools used is the DASH tool (Domestic Abuse, Stalking, Harassment and Honour Based Violence Assessment) which is part of the Multi-Agency Risk Assessment Coordinator referral. Currently, the DASH risk assessment form does not reflect the area of coercive control appropriately and needs to be adapted accordingly. It is, however, the tool that is used by most agencies. The purpose of the checklist provided is to provide a consistent and simple tool for practitioners who work with adult victims and survivors of domestic abuse in order to help them identify those who are at high risk of harm and whose cases should be referred to a Multi-Agency Risk Assessment Conference (MARAC) in order to manage their risk. It determines which cases should be referred to MARAC and what other support might be required. A completed form becomes an active record that can be referred to in future for case management. There are 27 questions that are put to the individual. The questions need to be asked in a sensitive and understanding way and the PSNI need to invest in training its officers to be able to

Taking Learnings From Other Jurisdictions 105

facilitate this process to obtain better information. Sensitively asking specific questions is critical because women are unlikely to volunteer this information on their own. In Women's Aid practitioner-led work, it is important to be creative and think carefully about the use of language.

In its 2019 report on the handling of domestic violence and abuse cases by the criminal justice system in NI, Criminal Justice Inspection Northern Ireland (2019, p. 8) commented that risk assessment in such cases could be improved, stating that:

> [T]he key issue in this risk assessment was the use of the DASH risk checklist; the PSNI had a high completion rate of these checklists, but the quality of the completed forms had been noted as a cause for concern with inconsistent supervision of the content of the form. Issues raised with the DASH checklist itself are not unique to Northern Ireland and the College of Policing was piloting a revised risk assessment tool.

As well as the PSNI, many other organisations complete the DASH risk assessment form including Women's Aid, other voluntary bodies and health and social care agencies. They need to know how to ask the questions and identify the risk associated with the questions to be able to support the individual. These questions need to be asked directly and the person asking the questions needs to be trauma-informed; this is essential for all those working with domestic abuse. Many of these women may still live with their partner, so repeat assault is a very high risk. Practitioners need to reflect on the importance of asking questions in a way that will elicit the truth. The right questioning and assessment tool could enable more disclosures at an earlier time, reducing risk and further harm.

It is evident that healthcare settings are not referring women into the system and appropriately screening for high, medium or low risk through this system. This is of great concern. During 2020/21, the MARAC statistics show that there were a total of 1,291 referrals. The majority of these came from the PSNI (840) and Women's Aid (233). No other voluntary sector agency made any referrals within this time frame which is also concerning. There were 198 referrals from health and social care, with the majority of these coming from children's social services and mental health services. There were no referrals from health visiting, midwifery, A & E or General Practitioners. This identifies a clear concern regarding different health and social care settings in relation to the knowledge of domestic abuse in all of its forms. There needs to be an investigation into the current models of training delivery within our local health and social care trusts, the screening obligations required in relation to domestic abuse and what the barriers are to screening and helping victims of domestic abuse within healthcare settings. There is a system in place for routine enquiry within maternity services in Northern Ireland, yet there were no referrals through to MARAC

106 *Sonya McMullan*

from any maternity services, health visiting or GP services. According to the Northern Ireland Statistics and Research Agency (2020, p. 9), there were 22,447 births in Northern Ireland in 2019. It is therefore very surprising that there were no referrals made from these services. The extreme demands on health services are understood and no apportioning of blame is intended. However, there is a need to review policies and procedures including training and awareness for all health professionals in relation to the assessment of domestic abuse victims. Minsky-Kelly et al. (2005) examined the barriers to domestic violence screening and referral in healthcare settings, and found that the main issues included time constraints and staff frustration. The researchers also found that:

> Other important recommendations include ongoing staff training, feedback to staff on patients who are helped, problem-solving privacy concerns with staff, and flexibility with when patients are screened to facilitate rapport with patients. This research also points to the potential for success in expanding screening procedures into outpatient settings rather than focusing largely on emergency departments. Outpatient providers may be better equipped to deal with [domestic violence] cases because of more long-standing relationships with patients. In addition, these providers may be able to provide more effective follow-ups than is feasible in acute care settings.
>
> (p. 1306)

A substantial amount of training is involved to ensure that DASH forms are completed accurately, as those completing the forms must consider how to ask the questions and then how to respond to the answers. Research by Barlow and Walklate (2021) focuses on the DASH form as a risk assessment tool and how it can adequately work in relation to capturing the offence of coercive control. They outline that there is clearly a need for improvement in relation to police training on coercive control and also guidance to police officers regarding the operation of the new piloted risk assessment tool which has taken place in England. 'However, the jury is still out on the extent to which an updated risk assessment tool will effectively shift police officers' focus from responding to what is measurable (i.e. incidents of physical violence) to process (i.e. coercive control) through an orientation to harm' (Barlow and Walklate, 2021, p. 900).

It is evident that training alone is not enough to identify, recognise and respond to domestic abuse appropriately. It is important to be able to ask questions in the right manner and establish trust and a relationship with the victim. A true understanding of what domestic abuse looks like in all its forms, encompassing coercive and controlling behaviours and the impact on the individual, is essential.

Public Perceptions and Attitudes

One of the major challenges is public perception and attitudes to domestic abuse. It is vitally important that awareness of the new offence becomes widespread, so that it is recognised in society that coercive and controlling behaviours are now a crime. One of the survivors who participated in the 'Hear Her Voice' project commented:

> Educat[e] schoolteachers to spot children, you know, everything. Educate everybody, everybody, in every walk of life: Managers, businesses, everyone . . . get it out everywhere. Into every workplace. Use it to educate people and get it out on the social media platforms, and 'like' and 'share'. People need to know that this is still happening in this world, and people need to know that you don't have to accept it. And you shouldn't be doing this if you are the perpetrator, you know? It's just a matter of getting so many people to know that this is going on.
>
> (Women's Aid NI, 2021B, p. 65)

Children and young people learn in so many places, and not just in the classroom. For instance, popular culture educates in its own ways, and it often sends contradictory messages as to what constitutes 'love'. As Snyder has argued:

> We cannot simply dump this on schools that are already under-resourced with teachers who are overworked. Systemic change cannot be ad hoc. And how are young people to learn what morbid jealousy looks like when our popular media frames stalking as romantic? When the Twilight movies, for example, portray romance as a man watching over a woman as she sleeps?
>
> (2020, p. 290)

It is hoped that the creation of a domestic abuse offence will remove the ambiguity regarding how domestic abuse is talked about in public and in the media. Women's Aid NI recognises the work that the media can do and the responsibility they hold:

> How the media reports on domestic violence and abuse informs how we as a society respond to it as a criminal act and to how we treat those who fall victim to it. Our response to victims of domestic violence and abuse determines how that person moves forward. A good responsible response to domestic violence and abuse, where the survivor is believed and supported, can enable that person to move on from the abuse they have suffered. A bad response, where their suffering is minimised, or their abuser is defended can re-traumatise a survivor and obstruct their recovery.
>
> (2020, p. 4)

108 Sonya McMullan

For the public to recognise a crime they need to know that it is a crime, so more public awareness is needed across the board. Public awareness can lead to prevention of abuse and also information on pathways to support victims. This is essential if we want people to recognise these behaviours.

Women's Aid strongly believes that preventative education needs to be a continuous journey with children and young people receiving clear messages about keeping safe from a young age. Education programmes should start in preschool with confidence building and teaching about respect for one another and this should be reinforced and further expanded upon as a child or young person progresses to primary and post-primary levels. It is only when children and young people are fully educated about these serious issues that we will see real change.

Prosecution

Prior to the new domestic abuse offence, there was no way of prosecuting domestic abuse specifically in Northern Ireland (see further Chapters 1 and 2 of this volume). Domestic abuse in itself was never previously a criminal act. However, all criminal justice agencies now need to have a better understanding of coercive control as referred to earlier. Women's Aid developed training for both the PSNI and the PPS prior to this offence becoming operational. This has been a great model of partnership working. The PSNI training involved working closely with colleagues at the PSNI Training College in Garnerville and we produced an online training programme consisting of four modules outlining the new offence and bringing in the voices of victims and survivors within the training package. This was mandatory for all serving police officers in Northern Ireland to complete. The PSNI Training recently won an award at the PSNI Problem Solving Awards which was a huge achievement and acknowledgement of the work done.

There is an increasing understanding that perpetrators employ a range of behaviours over a period of time that undermines the victim's autonomy and his or her capacity to make decisions. Within Women's Aid, this is witnessed in the daily work through survivors' voices and sharing their stories of what coercive control looks like to them. The perpetrator may use a combination of physical and non-physical, and criminal and non-criminal tactics amounting to a pattern of behaviour that regulates all aspects of their lives, with refusals to cooperate leading to punishment. This is difficult for criminal justice agencies to understand, and it involves a vastly different kind of policing, for example, as compared to responding to a physical assault. Police officers must identify the offence and then of course collect enough evidence to bring the case forward for prosecution (see further Chapters 3 and 4 of this volume). There has always been an issue of women withdrawing statements (Cretney and Davis, 1997) and not wanting to proceed for many reasons and this will also be the case as regards the new offence unless there are fundamental changes put in place.

Taking Learnings From Other Jurisdictions 109

Walklate et al. (2018) suggested that policing would not be able to adapt to the new conceptualisation of domestic abuse as an ongoing pattern of abuse driven by uneven distributions of power within a relationship. In addition, the absence of physical evidence could allow perpetrators even more latitude to present these crimes to attending officers as 'overreacting' and to convince officers that no crime has taken place, as observed in cases of stalking and harassment (Taylor-Dunn et al., 2021).

Women's Aid submitted a Freedom of Information request to the PPS in October 2020 with regard to the number of prosecutions in domestic abuse cases in NI. There were 31,817 domestic abuse incidents reported to the PSNI between April 2020 and May 2021. Out of that figure, 8,360 domestic abuse crimes were reported to the PPS by PSNI, and 2,968 suspects of domestic abuse offences were prosecuted.[5] NI does not have a good rate of prosecutions in relation to domestic abuse cases and this is concerning moving forward with a domestic abuse offence in relation to which gathering of evidence and witness statements will be more difficult (see further Chapter 6 of this volume).

There is a need for better evidence to be produced to enable more cases to go through the criminal justice system. There needs to be appropriate investment in training for the PSNI, and all legal professionals including the PPS and the judiciary. The appointment of an independent advocate to support the victim would encourage fewer withdrawals of statements. The acknowledgement that the majority of people coming into contact with our criminal justice system are in some way traumatised is key. As Gerry (2021, p. 18) comments,

> A 'fully trauma driven response' may be unachievable, but greater acknowledgement of the pervasiveness of trauma, the challenges it presents and the ways in which participation in the criminal justice process can come at the cost of individual therapeutic recovery, provides a mandate for further reform as a whole of justice approach.

Criminal Justice Inspection Northern Ireland (2019) has highlighted the issues around outcomes in cases of domestic abuse cases with many people withdrawing from the process. The issue of recanting is difficult and complex but contributes to low prosecutions of domestic abuse cases.

> In terms of outcomes recorded by the police, three in five offences committed in a domestic context did not progress to prosecution due to evidential difficulties and in more than two fifths, the victim did not wish to engage with/support or continue to support the criminal justice process. Data collected for this inspection suggests that around a third of cases did not meet the evidential or public interest tests required to proceed to a prosecution and just under a third resulted in a conviction at court. This inspection

110   *Sonya McMullan*

considered the approach of the criminal justice system in handling cases of domestic violence and abuse.

(Criminal Justice Inspection Northern Ireland, 2019, p. 7)

The ASSIST Project has been commissioned by the Department of Justice and the PSNI. ASSIST NI is a Northern Ireland wide advocacy service passionate about supporting victims of domestic and sexual abuse. They provide guidance, support and information; work with other service providers; and advocate on the victim's behalf. The ASSIST NI advocacy service is available to victims of domestic and sexual abuse whose details have been shared by the police as well as those referred by the Rowan Sexual Assault Referral Centre or from a MARAC meeting.[6] However, there is a gap in services as regards someone who can attend court with a victim of domestic abuse and support them through the process. The Gillen Review into the Law and Procedures in Serious Sexual Offences[7] recommended the introduction of an independent advocate and legal advice for victims/witnesses in serious sexual assault cases. Consequently, in March 2021, the Department of Justice announced the launch of a pilot scheme to provide publicly funded independent legal advice to victims of sexual offences, which would provide adult complainants with access to fully qualified Sexual Offences Legal Advisors (SOLAs).[8] Independent domestic violence advocates (IDVA) are an important feature in England and Wales, facilitating multi-agency working by liaising between agencies and the victim (Robinson and Payton, 2016). Therefore, introduction of independent advocates in NI, as has been piloted in the context of sexual assault cases, would be an important means of supporting the implementation of the new offence. Supporting a woman through the criminal justice system from the start of the justice process through to the end of the trial via an advocate would help to reduce withdrawals and enable more women to attend the court proceedings, which Taylor-Dunn (2015) has shown affects the advice defence lawyers give to their clients. An investment into advocacy-based services could save the public purse money in the long run.

Conclusion

If this new offence is to succeed in terms of reducing domestic abuse, much work is needed in all of the areas identified in this chapter, but most important is listening to the voice of the survivor. As Burman and Brooks-Hay (2018) likewise comment regarding the offence of coercive control in Scotland, the intention of the new legislation is to better reflect the experiences of victims of domestic abuse and improve the criminal justice system and access to that justice. As they conclude, however,

Legislative change cannot on its own lead to improvements. Whatever laws we have will be only as effective as those who enforce, prosecute, and apply them. Improving these practices – through education, training

Taking Learnings From Other Jurisdictions 111

and embedding best practice and domestic abuse expertise – is likely to be more effective than the creation of new offences alone.

(Burman and Brooks-Hay, 2018, p. 11)

The new legislation has brought NI into line with the rest of the UK and through thorough research and consultation, NI has taken learnings from these other jurisdictions. However, to truly succeed and overcome the challenges, there needs to be a societal shift in attitudes towards domestic abuse, through education and public awareness and true investment. The reality is that domestic abuse ruins lives and opportunities for children and young people, and investment in early intervention and prevention is essential. NI has a real opportunity to move forward with this new legislation to better inform our criminal justice agencies and health and social care providers to implement change. We truly need to listen to victims and survivors in this regard.

Notes

1 Women's Aid NI, www.womensaidni.org/what-is-domestic-abuse/coercive-control/.
2 Women's Aid NI, www.womensaidni.org/press-release-womens-aid-launch-a-petition-for-a-violence-against-women-and-girls-strategy-in-ni/.
3 Executive Office Northern Ireland, www.executiveoffice-ni.gov.uk/topics/ending-violence-against-women-and-girls).
4 Women's Aid NI, www.womensaidni.org/hear-her-voice/about-hear-her-voice/.
5 This information was provided to Women's Aid Federation NI by the PPS Information and Policy Unit via a Freedom of Information Act (2000) request (FOI 697–20/21).
6 ASSIST NI, https://assistni.org.uk/.
7 Gillen Review: Report into the law and procedures in serious sexual offences in Northern Ireland, 9 May 2019, www.justice-ni.gov.uk/sites/default/files/publications/justice/gillen-report-may-2019.pdf.
8 Department of Justice, 'Justice Minister launches scheme to provide free legal advice to victims of sexual offences', 31 March 2021, www.justice-ni.gov.uk/news/justice-minister-launches-scheme-provide-free-legal-advice-victims-sexual-offences.

References

Aldridge, J. (2021) '"Not an Either/or Situation": The Minimization of Violence Against Women in United Kingdom "Domestic Abuse" Policy', *Violence Against Women*, 27, pp. 1823–1839.
Barlow, C. and Walklate, S. (2021) 'Gender, Risk Assessment and Coercive Control: Contradictions in Terms?', *The British Journal of Criminology*, 61, pp. 887–904.
Burman, M. and Brooks-Hay, O. (2018) 'Aligning Policy and Law? The Creation of a Domestic Abuse Offence Incorporating Coercive Control', *Criminology and Criminal Justice*, 18, pp. 67–83.
Cretney, A. and Davis, G. (1997) 'Prosecuting Domestic Assault: Victims Failing Courts, or Courts Failing Victims?', *Howard Journal*, 36, pp. 146–157.
Criminal Justice Inspection Northern Ireland (2019) 'No Excuse – Public Protection Inspection II: A Thematic Inspection of the Handling of Domestic Violence and

112 *Sonya McMullan*

Abuse Cases by the Criminal Justice System in Northern Ireland', https://cjini.org/getattachment/798d1207-6bd0-4173-a933-34583669ec88/facts.aspx.

Department of Health, Social Services and Public Safety and Department of Justice (2016) 'Stopping Domestic and Sexual Violence and Abuse in Northern Ireland – A Seven Year Strategy', www.justice-ni.gov.uk/sites/default/files/publications/doj/stopping-domestic-sexual-violence-ni.pdf.

Gerry, F. (2021) 'Trauma Informed Courts', *New Law Journal*, 171(7922), pp. 16–18.

Minsky-Kelly, D., Hamberger, L.K., Pape, D.A. and Wolff, M. (2005) 'We've Had Training, Now What? Qualitative Analysis of Barriers to Domestic Violence Screening and Referral in a Health Care Setting', *Journal of Interpersonal Violence*, 20, pp. 1288–1309.

Myhill, A. (2015) 'Measuring Coercive Control: What Can We Learn from National Population Surveys?', *Violence against Women*, 21, pp. 355–375.

Northern Ireland Statistics and Research Agency (2020) 'Registrar General Northern Ireland Annual Report', www.nisra.gov.uk/sites/nisra.gov.uk/files/publications/RG%20Annual%20Report%202019.PDF.

ONS (2019) 'Domestic Abuse and the Criminal Justice System, England and Wales: November 2019', www.ons.gov.uk/peoplepopulationandcommunity/crimeandjustice/articles/domesticabuseandthecriminaljusticesystemenglandandwales/november2019.

PSNI (2022) 'Domestic Abuse Incidents and Crimes Recorded by the Police in Northern Ireland, Update to 30th June 2022', www.psni.police.uk/sites/default/files/2022-09/domestic-abuse-bulletin-jun_-22_0.pdf.

Robinson, A. and Payton, J. (2016) 'Independent Advocacy and Multi-Agency Responses to Domestic Violence', in Hilder, S. and Bettinson, V. (eds.) *Domestic Violence: Interdisciplinary Perspectives on Protection, Prevention and Intervention*. London: Palgrave, pp. 249–272.

Snyder, R.L. (2020) *No Visible Bruises*. London: Scribe UK.

Taylor-Dunn, H. (2015) 'The Impact of Victim Advocacy on the Prosecution of Domestic Violence Offences: Lessons from a Realistic Evaluation', *Criminology and Criminal Justice*, 16, pp. 21–39.

Taylor-Dunn, H., Bowen, E. and Gilchrist, E.A. (2021) 'Reporting Harassment and Stalking to the Police: A Qualitative Study of Victims' Experiences', *Journal of Interpersonal Violence*, 36, https://journals.sagepub.com/doi/10.1177/0886260518811423.

Waalen, J., Goodwin, M.M., Spitz, A.M., Petersen, R. and Saltzman, L.E. (2000) 'Screening of Intimate Partner Violence by Health Care Providers: Barriers and Interventions', *American Journal of Preventive Medicine*, 19, pp. 230–237.

Walklate, S., Fitz-Gibbon, K. and McCulloch, J. (2018) 'Is More Law the Answer? Seeking Justice for Victims of Intimate Partner Violence Through the Reform of Legal Categories', *Criminology and Criminal Justice*, 18, pp. 115–131.

Women's Aid NI (2020) 'Responsible Reporting Matters: Media Guidelines for Reporting on Domestic Abuse', www.womensaidni.org/assets/uploads/2020/11/Responsible-Reporting-Matters-2020-2.pdf.

Women's Aid NI (2021A) 'Unlocking Potential – Building on Success', https://www.womensaidni.org/resources/the-womens-aid-strategy-plan-2022-2025/#:~:text=This%20change%20road%20map%20details,over%20a%203%20year%20period.

Women's Aid NI (2021B) 'Women's Aid Federation NI Annual Report: 2020/2021', www.womensaidni.org/assets/uploads/2021/12/WAFNI-Annual-Report-20-21.pdf.

Index

ASSIST NI advocacy service 110

'bad character' 75–76, 91
body worn video 50, 58, 59, 60, 61, 73
British/ Irish Council 3
British/ Irish Governmental
    Conference 3

children 25, 33, 50, 52, 68, 77, 99, 100,
    104, 105, 107, 108, 111
Council of Europe Convention on
    Preventing and Combating
    Violence Against Women and
    Domestic Violence (Istanbul
    Convention) 1, 5, 14, 15
COVID-19 pandemic 51, 68
Crime Survey of England and Wales 34,
    81, 101
Criminal Justice Inspection Northern
    Ireland (CJINI) 3, 105,
    109–110
Crown Court 66, 77
Crown Prosecution Service (CPS) 57,
    70, 82, 85, 94

DASH risk assessment 104–105, 106
defences to domestic abuse offence
    27–28
Digital Media Investigators 60
domestic homicide reviews 7–8, 59–60
Domestic Violence and Abuse Disclosure
    Scheme 7

European Convention on Human Rights
    5, 66, 74, 75
European Court of Human Rights 5, 74
European Union 3, 66

gendered approach to domestic abuse 34,
    100–102
Gillen Review 67, 68, 70, 77, 110
Good Friday Agreement (Belfast
    Agreement) 3

harassment 17, 53
hearsay 71–75, 76
Her Majesty's Inspectorate of
    Constabulary 45
Home Office 34

independent domestic violence
    advocates 110

Law Commission for England and
    Wales 72
Long, Naomi MLA 7, 8, 21, 23, 24, 25,
    28, 29

Magistrates' Court 34, 66
mens rea 26–27
Multi-Agency Risk Assessment
    Conference (MARAC) 3, 104,
    105–106, 110
myths surrounding domestic abuse
    76–77

National Council of Police 70
non-fatal strangulation 8, 50, 56
Northern Ireland Assembly 3, 4, 7, 13,
    15, 21, 23, 24, 25, 28, 29, 102
Northern Ireland Assembly Committee
    for Justice 25, 27
Northern Ireland Department of Health,
    Social Services and Public
    Safety 3, 16, 101

114 *Index*

Northern Ireland Department of Justice 3, 6, 13, 14, 15, 16, 17, 24, 27, 28, 70, 101, 104, 110
Northern Ireland Executive 3, 101, 102
Northern Ireland Office 3, 101
Northern Ireland Protocol 3
North/ South Ministerial Council 3

penalties for domestic abuse offence 28, 66
Police Scotland 26
Police Service of Northern Ireland (PSNI) 4, 7, 41, 54, 55, 58–59, 60, 99, 104, 105, 108, 109, 110
police training 9, 26, 45, 50–61, 87–88, 104–105, 106, 108, 110–111
pre-charge considerations 85–89
pre-charge disclosure 87–89
Public Prosecution Service (PPS) 66, 70, 82, 85, 87, 94, 104, 108, 109

rapid video response 50, 58, 59, 60, 61
reporting of domestic abuse 40, 51, 52, 56, 81–82, 99, 109

Sentencing Council 87
societal awareness 4, 15, 53, 81, 107–108, 111

special measures 69
stalking 8, 56
'Stopping Domestic and Sexual Violence and Abuse in Northern Ireland' strategy 3–4, 6, 16, 102

'Tackling Violence at Home' strategy 3, 101
the 'Troubles' 2–3

United Nations Committee on the Elimination of Discrimination Against Women (CEDAW Committee) 2, 5–6
United Nations Convention on the Elimination of All Forms of Discrimination Against Women (CEDAW) 2, 5

victim personal statement 86
Victims' Charter 66
Victoria, Australia 46
Violence Against Women and Girls Strategy (Northern Ireland) 101, 102

Westminster Parliament 3, 4
Women's Aid 5, 10, 20, 36, 99–111